COCONUT OIL RECIPES

Carl Preston

COCONUT OIL RECIPES

Coconut Maple Granola

Coconut Maple Granola is the best snacking granola.

Composition
- 3 cups rolled oats
- 3/4 cup natural almonds
- 1/4 cup unsweetened coconut flakes
- 1/2 cup unsweetened shredded coconut
- 1/2 cup coconut oil
- 1/2 cup maple syrup
- 1/4 cup brown sugar
- 1 teaspoon kosher salt

Instruction
1. Preheat the oven up to 350F.
2. Put all the constituents into a sizable container and add oats, almonds, the two forms of coconut, coconut oil, and at this point add coconut oil as well as the maple syrup on top and mix.
3. Once fully mixed then, put the brown sugar also and keep on mixing.
4. Finally, add in the salt and then complete the stirring.
5. Now, disperse the granola in a uniform surface on a big rimmed food preparation sheet and then place in the oven for about 25 to 30 minutes ensuring to keep turning the granola at regular intervals or something like that.
6. Allow the granola cool and then use an air sealed container to store or keep it. Note: It properly stored, it can last two weeks.

Toasted Coconut Waffles with Maple Cream

Coconut waffles are certainly enjoyable with maple sweetened whipped -= beaten cream along with a ample maple syrup sprinkle.

Ingredients

- 1/2 cup of either sweetened or even unsweetened chopped coconut
- 4 tsp of coconut oil
- 5 sizeable eggs
- 1/2 cup of agave nectar
- 1 teaspoon of fresh vanilla extract
- 1/4 teaspoon salt
- 1/2 teaspoon baking soda
- 1/3 cup of coconut flour
- 2 tsps of crushed bananas
- 1/4 cup unsweetened toasted coconut chips

For the maple cream

- 1/2 cup of full cream
- 2. tsps of natural maple syrup

Guidance

1. Preheat to 350°F.
2. Just position a tray in the middle of oven.
3. Now, put your coconut on a baking tray in the oven and up to 4 minutes. Always, watch over the coconut lest it burns when it turns brown.
4. Take off the toasted coconut from the oven and keep it aside.
5. Use an average size bowl to mix the eggs, vanilla extract, coconut oil, agave nectar and the pulpy bananas together. Continue mixing until everything is nicely combined.
6. At this point, use one small dish to mix the coconut flour, baking soda and salt.
7. You can use your fingers to mix everything so that the coconut flour does not get lumps.
8. Now, mix the dry constituents into the moisten components. The combination starts to thicken just as you continue to mix. Put the toasted, shredded coconut and then mix to combine very well.
9. Let the mixture to stay like five minutes however you should preheat the waffle metal.
10. Depending on the size of waffle iron, put on waffle sheets and bake.
11. To prepare your maple cream,, you should blend the maple syrup and full cream together in a moderate bowl, till it softs.
12. Serve the baked waffle warm together with toasted coconut flakes and maple cream.

Super Soggy Banana Bread

Constituents

- 2 cups of flour
- 1 1/3 teaspoon baking soda
- 3 medium-sized bananas
- 1 1/2 teaspoon baking powder
- little of kosher salt
- 1 virgin coconut oil or butter
- 2 cups of yogurt cheese or use cream cheese
- 3/4 cups of brown sugar
- 2 egg

Instruction

1. Preheat oven to 350F.
2. Use parchment to line your bread pan.
3. Use a fine mesh to sift all the dry constituents into a sizable mixing bowl and keep it aside.
4. Use another mixing bowl to blend the coconut oil or perhaps butter for about 3 minutes until it's soft.
5. Include the yogurt cheese, while you continue mixing on medium speed for about another 3 minutes.
6. Put in sugar and continue mixing for 5 minutes or until fluffy.
7. Bring in bananas and egg and blend to form mixture.
8. Add the dry constituents and mix up for 3 minutes on medium speed until well mixed.
9. Now, put the dough into bread pan.
10. Put in the oven and bake for about 40 to 50 minutes or until golden brown. You can check buy piercing the bread with knife and it comes out clean
11. Serve. Enjoy!

Whole Wheat Pumpkin Muffins with Coconut Oil

Materials
- 5 tablespoons of high quality coconut oil
- 2 sizable eggs.
- 2/3 cups of sugar, evaporated cane juice crystals or simply packaged coconut palm sugar
- 8 oz of canned pumpkin
- 1 teaspoon vanilla extract
- 2 cups whole wheat flour
- 1 teaspoons of baking powder
- 1 teaspoon of grounded cinnamon
- 1 teaspoon pumpkin pie spice
- Little salt

Directions
1. Chopped almonds for topping (suggested)
2. Preheat oven to 375°F. Use paper to line the 6 muffin cups
3. Using electric mixer whisk the coconut oil together with the sugar and blend until properly combined. Now, add in these ingredients - pumpkin, vanilla and eggs, continue mixing until soft.
4. At this point, in a medium bowl, mix up together the flour, cinnamon, salt, baking powder and pumpkin pie spice and stir mixture into the pumpkin blend mix until well incorporated
5. Pour the batter into the 6 muffin cups (fill each cup to the top; spread the sliced almonds on top.
6. Bake at 375 for 23-25 Put the muffins in the oven and allow baking for about 22 to 25 minutes. When properly baked, allow to cool then eat.

Veggie lover Chocolate Cake

Ingredients
- 1 cup of generally useful flour
- 1/2 cup of whole wheat flour
- 1 cup of sugar or Rapadura
- 1 teaspoon baking soda
- 2/3 cup of unsweetened cocoa powder
- 1 teaspoon vanilla concentrate
- 1/4 teaspoon of sea salt
- 1 tablespoon apple juice vinegar
- 1/3 cup of virgin coconut oil, liquefied and cooled somewhat
- 1 cup of coconut water, or 3/4 cup of water and 1/4 glass coconut milk.

Preparation
1. Preheat oven to 350° F.
2. Oil a 9 by 13 inch baking pan with coconut oil and line the base with paper material to fit the cup.
3. Blend the dry fixings in a big blending dish. In a small dish, combine the coconut water, coconut oil, vanilla and vinegar. Empty the wet fixings into the dry constituents and speed until all around mixed and smooth.
4. Empty the mixture into the readied dish, bake in the oven for around 20 minutes and until brown or that when a toothpick is dipped into the center of the cake comes out neat.
5. Allow cake to cool totally on a rack. At that point, use clean blade to slide the edges of the cake to remove it from the pan. Now, place a sheet or big rectangular cutting board on top of the cake skillet. Hold the sides solidly and rapidly bring out the cake onto the board. Peel the paper from the underside of the cake and place the cake in the cooler or freezer to solidify. At this point

when the cake is firm, remove from freezer and cut into required shape.

6. On the off chance the heart shape appears hard; you can essentially cut the cake into square shape for a four-layer cake.
7. You can ice just in between the layers and use cocoa powder to dust on top.
8. And should you like all the more icing and sweetness, then accompanying formula should be enough to ice the top and sides also.
9. Vegetarian Coconut Milk Chocolate Fudge Icing
10. It's important to have your cake layers prepared to ice before starting the icing because, it really will set rapidly.

Fixings
- 1/2 container virgin coconut oil
- 1 containers sugar
- 1/2 container unsweetened common cocoa powder
- 1/2 teaspoon ocean salt
- 1 container coconut milk
- 1 teaspoon of vanilla concentrate

1. In a medium thick bottomed frying pan, dissolve the coconut oil; add cocoa powder, sugar and salt and mix.
2. Include the coconut milk, mix well, and heat the blend to the point of boiling. Reduce heat to a steady yet slow boiling and allow cooking for about 5 minutes, mixing frequently until it thickens.
3. At this point remove from heat and then add in vanilla. Allow the mixture for like 25 minutes to cool.
4. Beat the icing with a wooden spoon until it thickens. Spread it over your cake layers.
5. Enjoy!

Dark Chocolate Brownies

INGREDIENTS

- 1 cup of fresh coconut oil
- 1 glass light cocoa sugar
- 5 ounces of good quality 60 to 70% cocoa chocolate
- 1/2 teaspoon fine ocean salt
- 1/2 cup of almond
- 1/4 cup of sorghum flour
- 1 tablespoon whiskey vanilla
- 1/4 teaspoon baking soda.
- 2 fresh eggs
- Discretionary: 1/2 cup of slashed walnuts or even pecans
- Dark chocolate chips for topping.

Directions

1. Preheat the stove to 350º F.
2. Using paper material to line 8 by 8 inch square baking container.
3. At this point, melt the coconut oil and the dark chocolate in a pot over low heat, gently mixing together to blend in.
4. Now mix the sorghum flour, brown sugar, sea salt, baking soda and almond meal together in a mixing bowl. Create a whole in the inside and pour in the melted dark chocolate mixture, beaten eggs and vanilla concentrate. Continue blending on low to medium speed for about two to three minutes until the mixture thickens and gets to be smooth and polished.
5. For those that love nuts, you can add in the nuts by hand and spread the batter into the readied baking tray. You can use silicone spatula to evenly spread out the batter.
6. Spread the dark chocolate chips on top and gently press in.
7. Put in the preheated oven at 350º F for about 30 to 35 minutes, or until it browns. You will notice that the top will break, similar to a flourless chocolate cake.
8. Allow to cool on a wire rack; then remove the cooled brownies from the skillet by pulling the foil edges.
9. Chill for 60 minutes before cutting.

Note: To have that chocolate-mint brownie, you can utilize 1 teaspoon of 1 teaspoon vanilla concentrate and peppermint concentrate.

Fluffy Coconut Cupcakes

CONSTITUENTS

For COCUNUT CUPCAKES
- 2 cups general flour
- 1 cup of sugar
- 1 teaspoon of baking powder
- 1 teaspoon baking soda
- ½ teaspoon salt
- 1 cup of coconut milk
- ½ cup of canola oil
- 2 tablespoons of vanilla concentrate
- 1 tablespoon of apple cider or white vinegar

For COCONUT FROSTING
- 1 cup of unrefined coconut oil (solid at room temperature)
- 3 cups of sugar
- 1 teaspoon of fresh vanilla extract
- 4 tablespoons of coconut milk or any nondairy milk.

For Garnishing:
- use 2 cups of chopped coconut

Direction

1. Preheat the oven to 350° F.
2. Use cupcake liners to line cupcake pans.
3. Mix the flour, baking powder, sugar, salt and baking soda together in a bowl. In a different mixing bowl, mix your coconut oil vanilla, vinegar and coconut milk.
4. Now, add the dry mixture into the wet blend and continue mixing until properly mixed. Note never over mix.
5. Pour the batter into lined cupcake just about 2/3 full.
6. Put in the oven and bake for about 15 to 18 minutes, or simply check by piercing through the cake at the middle with a toothpick thus, if it's clean when pulled out with some crumbs clinging to it. Then remove from oven and allow to cool.
7. Let the cupcakes cool completely before applying the icing.
8. Now, prepare the Coconut Frosting:
9. With the help of a portable or standing food processor, blend the coconut oil until silky.
10. Reduce the mixer speed, and then add in vanilla, sugar and 1 tablespoon of coconut milk one at time as much as you need to, until frosting has reached a spreadable uniformity.
11. Increase the mixer speed for 2 minutes until it's soft and smooth.

Coconut Oil Peanut Butter Cookies

Constituents

- 3 cups of flour
- 2 cup of coconut oil
- 3/4 cup of sugar
- 1 tsp baking soda
- 1 tsp vanilla concentrate
- 1/3 cup cocoa sugar
- 1 tsp heating powder
- 1 tsp salt
- 2 cups Crunchy unsalted peanut spread
- 3 eggs or 2 big sized ones)
- 1 tsp of cinnamon
- Optional, should you like Omega Vitamins, then, add a teaspoon or maybe two spoons of hemp oil to the coconut oil. This will add new nutty taste.

INSTRUCTION

1. Preheat to 350° F.
2. Mix all the dry fixings together, - flour, baking soda, salt, baking powder and cinnamon. Put aside
3. Mix the butter and coconut oil together.
4. Beat in the eggs.
5. Include the sugars and vanilla.
6. Add the dry fixings. You can use your hands to roll into little balls and then utilize potato masher to make cross-hash design.
7. Bake for chewy treats for around 10 minutes but more for crunchy.

Nikki's Wholesome Cookie Recipe

Active Ingredients
- 3 big ripened bananas. Properly mashed (1 1/2 cups)
- 1/2 cup of coconut oil slightly warm and not solid (or olive oil)
- 2 cups of rolled oats
- 1 teaspoon of vanilla concentrate.
- 1/2 cup of almond meal
- 1/3 cup of unsweetened nicely chopped coconut
- 1/2 teaspoon of cinnamon
- 1/4 teaspoon of sea salt
- 1 teaspoon of baking powder
- 6 ounces of chocolate chips or maybe sliced dark chocolate bar

Instruction
1. Preheat oven to 350° F.
2. Mix together the coconut oil, vanilla concentrate and mashed bananas in a big bowl and keep safe.
3. In a different bowl, mix the chopped coconut, baking powder, almond meal, oats and salt. Now, combine the two mixtures and mix until well blended. Retract the chocolate chunks. If the dough is kind of looser unlike the normal cookie dough, never fret about it. Place the dollops of the dough onto a paper lined baking sheet, each one just about 2 teaspoons in proportions and an inch in space.
4. Bake for 12 to 16 mins.
5. Simply remove from heat and serve.

Coconut Butter Blondies with Coconut Buttercream Frosting

Blondies preparation
Constituents
- 1 cup of Artisana Coconut Butter
- 3 omega 3 eggs
- 6 Medjool dates
- 1/4 tsp of sea salt
- 1/2 tsp of baking soda
- 1 1/2 tsp of pure vanilla concentrate
- 3 drops of liquid stevia concentrate
- 1/2 cup of chopped walnuts

Date preparation
- 6 Medjool dates, pitted
- 1/2 tsp of pure vanilla extract
- 1 tsp of coconut oil

Procedure
1. Preheat oven to 325° F.
2. Mix with a hand mixer, vanilla extract, eggs, baking soda and salt together in a medium sized bowl.
3. Incorporate 1 cup of coconut oil and then stir the mixture with a spatula until smooth.
4. Bring in the date mixture
5. Toss in 3 droplets of liquid stevia.
6. As you stir the batter, bring in the sliced walnuts and also keep mixing up until uniformly spread.
7. Carefully oil with coconut oil a 9 by 9 pyrex baking tray.
8. Put the batter into baking tray and bake in the preheated oven for about 21 to 30 minutes. until brown

To make the dates for the batter
1. Slice dates in two and then take out the pit.
2. Put into a microwave safe dish, add 3 tablespoons of water.
3. Put in the microwave for 32 seconds and then mash with a fork.
4. Put in 1/2 tsp of vanilla concentrate, 1 tablespoon of coconut oil and keep mashing with the fork.
5. Add more tablespoon of water, then microwave for about 30 seconds more and also mix.

Coconut Buttercream Frosting
Components
- 1 cup of natural palm shortening.
- 1 tsp of organic vanilla extract.
- 3 tablespoons of coconut milk.
- 1 full dropper of liquid stevia.
- 1/4 cup of chopped coconut.

Method
1. Mix the palm shortening with hand mixer until soft and smooth
2. Incorporate the vanilla concentrate, coconut milk, liquid stevia and keep on mixing.
3. When the mixture is uniformly blended, then gently add the chopped coconut using a spatula.
4. Note: you have to use the frosting right away or put in a refrigerator till when needed. Prior to spreading the frosting, let it dissolve at room temperature.

Instruction
1. Let the blondies to get cool before placing the frosting.
2. After frosting, you can then cut into squares.
3. Serve and enjoy!

Coconut Beef & Broccoli Rice Bowls

Contents

- 2 cups of delicious sticky rice
- 1 cup of coconut milk
- 2 cups of water
- 3 tbsp of coconut oil
- 1 pound of flat iron or finely cut beefsteak
- 1 shallot, diced
- 3 garlic cloves, diced
- 2. tbsp of soy sauce
- 1 big head broccoli, slash into little florets
- tbsp of Thai seasoning
- 2 tsp of carefully grated natural ginger
- 1 cup of coconut milk
- 1/2 tablespoon of lime juice
- tbsp of full brown sugar
- Garden-fresh cilantro, for topping
- Toasted sesame seeds, for garnish

Instructions

1. Add 1 1/2 cups cold water into the rice in a bowl, cover and put in the fridge for 5-7 hours.
2. Put rice together with the water into a saucepan. Add in coconut milk and allow it to steam on medium heat. Cover the pot and lower heat to low - medium and let it simmer for ten minutes until rice is cooked and the water dried. Remove from heat and still covered for maybe 3 minutes.
3. When the rice is cooking, add in the cut beefsteak together with Thai seasoning.
4. Warm a tbsp of coconut oil in a big skillet and heat on medium-high heat. Put in 1/3 of cut beef, dispersing into a small layer. Fry until beef turns brown. Move to a dish. Fry the left over beef and add more coconut oil into the skillet when you need more.
5. Put the pot on heat again, if required, you can pour in more oil though the leftover oil drippings from the beef ought to be adequate. Bring in shallot, ginger, garlic and fry for about 28 seconds until the great aroma comes
6. Put in broccoli and continue frying for 2 to 3 minutes until shiny green. Include coconut milk, sugar, lime juice and soy sauce, allow simmering for about 2 minutes or when broccoli is soft and sauce is thickens Add in beef and keep stirring to uniformly cover with sauce.
7. Serve rice, and to with broccoli beef mixture.
8. Also, spray fresh cilantro on it as well as sesame seeds. Enjoy!

Apple-Coconut Oil Crisp

Contents

For the apples
- 2. tbsp of almond flour
- 4 Cut Opal apples
- 1 tsp of cinnamon

For the topping
- ½ cup of almond flour
- 1¼ cup of rolled oats
- 1/2 cup of coconut oil
- 1 cup of honey
- 1 cup of sliced pecans
- 1/4 teaspoon salt
- 1 tsp of cinnamon

Directions
1. Oil about 9 by 13 baking pan. Moreover, preheat the oven to 350o Add the apples together with cinnamon, almond flour and spread uniformly in a layer
2. Beat together the coconut oil and honey until smooth. In a big bowl, mix the pecans, rolled oats, salt, almond flour and cinnamon. Stir in honey and coconut oil mixture.
3. Empty the oat mixture on the apples uniformly cover it and bake for 30-40 minutes and the topping should be lightly brown.
4. Allow to cool for about 14 - 20 minutes.
5. Serve..

Peanut Butter-Chocolate, Coconut with Almonds and Apples

Contents
- 1 tbsp of chopped dark chocolate or even chocolate chips
- 1 average sweet apple
- 1/2 teaspoon of coconut oil or alternatively canola oil
- 1 tbsp of sweetened coconut flakes
- 1 tbsp of quality peanut butter or alternatively any nut butter
- 1 tablespoon of chopped toasted almonds

Directions
1. Wash apple and cut to pieces onto a dish.
2. Add the oil and chocolate in one small microwave safe container and then heat until it dissolves and becomes smooth. In a different dish, melt peanut butter until smooth and light enough to drops.
3. Pour the chocolate-peanut butter on apples. Add in almonds and coconut.

Bang Bang Cauliflower

Contents

- 1 Cup of unsweetened shredded or flakes coconut
- 1 Head cauliflower
- Salt & pepper
- 1 tbsp of garlic powder
- Diced Green onions
- 1 tbsp of Greek yogurt
- 3 tbsp of coconut oil
- 1 tsp of siracha
- 1 tsp of rice wine vinegar
- 2 tbsp of honey
- 1 tbsp of sweetened shredded coconut powder (optional)

Instructions

1. Do preheat the oven to 350°. Cut the cauliflower florets.
2. Add to the florets, 2 tablespoons of coconut oil, pepper, salt and garlic powder. Bake for about 20 minutes, ensuring that the coconut is adhering to the florets.
3. Whisk together in a different bowl, the yogurt, honey, siracha, rice wine vinegar, and 1 tablespoon of coconut oil until altogether mixed and smooth. Just increase siracha or honey
4. Take out the cauliflower from the oven and then top with green onions, one tablespoon of sweetened coconut and the leftover of coconut that are unable to stick on florets.
5. You can serve together with dipping sauce.

Chestnut Boss Snacks

Contents
- 1 cup of chestnut flour
- 1 cup of oat flour
- 1 cup of of almond flour
- 2 tbsp of arrowroot starch
- 1 tsp of baking powder
- 1/2 tsp of salt
- 2 eggs
- 6 tbsp of coconut oil or butter
- 1/2 cup of sunflower seeds, thinly chopped
- 1/3 cup of maple syrup
- 1/2 cup of your preferred

Directions
1. Preheat oven to 350 o F. Mix the first 6 ingredients together in a bowl and stir very well to combine properly. Use a different bowl to mix the eggs, coconut oil and maple syrup together.
2. Combine dry ingredients to wet mixture and really mix with your palm to incorporate. Refrigerate dough for about 20 to 30 minutes.
3. Add in the nicely ground sunflower seeds into mixing container. The moment dough is chilled and firms. Use tablespoon to scoop and then roll in sunflower seeds to coat. Put a hole in each rolled dough and fill with your preferred jam.
4. Place the pastries on baking sheet lined with parchment and the bake for 10 to 17 minutes at 350o F until they're golden brown. Allow for about 10 minutes to cool.
5. Then Consume.

Carrot Cake Granola

Contents

For Dry ingredients
- 1 cup of shredded coconut
- 1 cup of almond meal
- 2 cups of rolled oats
- ½ cup of pecans, coarsely chopped
- 1 tsp of cinnamon
- 1 cup of walnuts coarsely cut
- 2/3 tsp of ground ginger
- ½ tsp of smashed garlic cloves
- 1 sizable or maybe 2 smaller carrots, peeled and grated
- ½ tsp nutmeg

Moist ingredients
- 1/2 cup of maple syrup
- 1 Cup of coconut oil

Directions

1. Preheat oven to 340o F
2. Cleanse and then rind the carrots; grate with a box grater or alternatively with the grater of food processor accessory.
3. Combine in a big bowl, carrot and other dry ingredients and stir together.
4. Put in the maple syrup and coconut oil mixture into a saucepan and place over low heat; stir until it dissolves and mix up. Combine with the dry ingredients.
5. Empty the combination into a parchment lined baking sheet and then bake for 18 - 26 minutes, turn it after 14 minutes.
6. Be mindful of the granola particularly within the closing 6 - 10 mins to ensure the sides will not burn.
7. Remove from oven properly cooked, Let it cool totally on the sheet.
8. Eat. Put the remaining in an air-tight jar and store.

Baked Cinnamon Apple Oatmeal Cups

Contents

- 2 cups of rolled oats (not quick oats)
- 2 tsp of crushed cinnamon
- 1 tsp of baking powder
- 5 tbsp of coconut sugar
- 1/2 tsp of kosher salt
- 1/4 tsp of crushed allspice (optional)
- 1 tsp of orange zest
- 1/4 tsp of crushed nutmeg
- 1 tbsp of coconut oil
- 2 cups of almond unsweetened almond milk
- 1 flax egg (mix 1 tbsp of flax meal together with 3 tbsp of water, allow it stay for ten minutes)
- 1 cup of chopped apples (optional, use a Gala and Granny Smith)
- 2 tsp of vanilla extract

Directions

1. Preheat your oven to 350°.
2. Squirt 12 muffin pans with baking oil.
3. Prepare the flax egg in a small bowl
4. Now mix together in a big mixing bowl the oats, baking powder, cinnamon, the spices, salt, sugar and nutmeg.
5. As the flax egg set, stir in the almond milk, orange zest and vanilla
6. Mix the moisten contents into the oat batter and then mix together to combine.
7. Include the chopped apples and continue to stir until properly mixed.
8. Scoop the batter into each one muffin cups and set them in the center rack of oven.
9. Allow to bake for about 20 to 25 minutes until they are ready.
10. Remove from oven, and take out muffin containers, place them on wire rack to cool
11. You may serve oatmeal cups right away or alternatively top with maple syrup along with some regular Greek yogurt or rather with dairy free yogurt.

Note: Preserve in the oatmeal cups by wrapping with flexible wrap and keep in a freezer bag.

Greek Yogurt Lemon Bars

Contents

For CRUST
- 1 cup of graham cracker crumbs
- 2 tbsp of unsalted dissolved butter or alternatively melted coconut oil

For Filling
- 6 ounces of brick-style soft cream cheese dissolved at room temperature
- 1 tbsp of lemon zest
- 2 big Eggland's eggs
- 3/4 cup of regular nonfat or alternatively low fat Greek yogurt
- 1 sizable egg yolk
- 1 tsp of vanilla concentrate
- 1/3 cup of coarse sugar
- 1/3 cup of fresh lemon juice

Instructions

1. Preheat oven at 300°F. Next, use a square baking pan of about 8" or 9", line the pan with parchment but leaving an overhang for easy removal of bars.

2. Prepare the crust: Combine together the graham cracker crumbs together with melted butter in a container and mix until combined. Spread the crust uniformly onto baking pan and put in the oven for 5 minutes. Take away from oven and keep aside.

3. Prepare the filling: With a handheld or maybe standing mixer that has whisk accessory, whisk the cream cheese in a large bowl at high speed until fully smooth. Also, on medium-high speed, whisk in yogurt to fully mix. Next, stir in the eggs yolk along with egg. Lastly, add in the lemon juice, vanilla extract, lemon zest and sugar.

4. Now, pour filling on the crust and bake for about 20 to 30 minutes until bars are set. (Take out from oven and carefully shake the pan to check if bars are ready) If ready, then place on a wire rack and let them cool before preserving in the fridge to cool for 3 hours or more.

5. Now that it's refrigerated, remove bars from cups by gently pulling up the parchment overhang. The Leftovers should be kept in the fridge for as long as 7 days.

6. Optional: you can serve with fresh fruit topping.

Note: It's better to make the bars a day or two ahead of time, then covered firmly and keep in the fridge until when to serve. Bars could be iced and preserved for about 2 to 3 months, but needs to defrost in the fridge prior to serving.

Coconut Oil Zucchini Bread

Contents

The Wet Contents
- 1/2 cup of melted coconut oil
- 2/3 cup of unsweetened apple sauce
- 1 tsp of vanilla
- 1 whisked egg
- 3 tbsp of maple syrup
- 2 cup of unsweetened almond milk

The Dry Ingredients
- 1 cup of unpacked sliced zucchini
- 1/2 tsp of baking powder
- 1 1/2 cups of white whole wheat flour
- 1/2 cup of coconut sugar
- ½ tsp of cinnamon
- 1/2 tsp of baking soda
- ⅛ tsp of salt

Directions

1. Set oven at 350ºF to preheat. Grease the bread pan with coconut oil and keep aside.
2. Mix the dry ingredients together in a mixing container, stir until properly mixed.
1. Use small cheese grater to slice zucchini. You have to press hard with your palms the chopped zucchini to squeeze out as much liquid as you can.
3. Combine the wet ingredients together in a big mixing bowl till properly mixed.
4. Next gradually incorporate the dry mixture to moist mixture mix very well until batter is totally mixed.
5. Fill bread pans with batter and then bake for about 50 minutes to cook.
6. Serve.

Coconut Banana Cream Pie

Contents

Walnut Crust
- 1 cup of walnuts
- 1 tbsp of water
- 1 cup of shredded coconut

For Coconut Banana Filling
- ½ cup of fresh cashews, Soak for 4 hrs
- 1 tbsp of dissolved coconut oil
- 1 tbsp of fresh lemon juice
- ½ tsp of vanilla concentrate
- ½ cup of shredded coconut
- Salt to taste
- 2 ripped bananas

For Chocolate Mousse
- 2 tbsp of maple syrup
- 2 tbsp of raw chocolate powder
- 1 cup of cashews, wet for 4 hrs
- 1 tsp of vanilla extract
- 1 cup of water
- 2 tbsp of melted coconut oil
- Salt

Directions

Prepare the crust:
1. Blend the shredded coconut and walnuts together in a food processor, add water and blend to obtain a smooth mixture. Gradually distribute mixture into 12 small muffin cups then press dough down to the base as well as the sides to shape. Put the muffin cups in freezer.

To prepare coconut filling:
2. Wash and rinse cashews, put into a food processor, add coconut oil and lemon juice; blend until smooth. Bring in bananas, vanilla extract and shredded coconut, blend further to combine. Then use spoon to put filling into the chilled crusts and put back into freezer until filling hardens.

To prepare chocolate mousse:
3. Mix together in a food processor the cashews, maple syrup and water until smooth. Put in cocoa powder, also add small salt, and blend to combine, gently add coconut oil and mix properly. Put your mousse in the fridge for about 10 to 15 minutes.

Finally, piece all together:
4. Using a butter knife, bring out coconut pies from muffin cups; spread the cooled mousse and banana chip on top.
5. Keep in freezer until when you want to serve.

Honey Roasted Almond Butter

Contents
- 3 cups of raw almonds
- 1 1/2 tbsp of melted coconut oil
- 3 tbsp of honey, or more
- 1/8 tsp of sea salt

Instructions
1. Preheat oven to 350°. Whisk together in a small bowl the coconut oil, salt and honey until properly combined. Now, put almonds in a different container, after that pour the honey mixture on almonds and stir to coat.
2. Pass on almonds onto a lined baking sheet, spread evenly on the sheet, and bake for about 15 minutes until properly ready. Ensure you turn once.
3. Remove from oven and allow for about 15 minutes to cool.
4. Finally, pour almonds and if any leftover honey mixture into a food processor and blend until it's buttery, add more honey and small salt if necessary.
5. Serve and keep the remaining in an airtight container and refrigerate. Enjoy!

Avocado Cooler Fudge

Constituents

- 1 cup of dark chocolate chips
- 1/4 glass coconut oil
- 1/4 glass coconut cream
- 1 tablespoon of cocoa powder
- Salt
- 1 ripe avocado
- kosher sea salt

Guidelines

- Dissolve and mix together over medium-low heat - in a little pan, mix the chocolate, coconut cream, coconut oil, salt and cocoa powder .
- Mix the avocado and dissolved chocolate blend in a food processor and blend until it's smooth.
- Pour into a lubed 8 by 8 inch glass heating dish. Sprinkle kosher salt on it. Put in the freezer for up to 60 minutes to solidify. Then, cut into squares and eat.
- You can store the remaining in the refrigerator in a sealed shut holder.

Green Bean Dish

Contents

- 1 tbsp of coconut oil or alternatively butter
- 2 lbs of green beans
- 2 cups of parsnips
- 1 red chopped onion
- 1 2/3 cups of mushrooms, chopped
- ¼ cup of dietary yeast
- 3 cloves of crushed garlic
- 2 cups of water
- ½ tsp of salt and pepper, to taste
- ½ tsp of ground red pepper (optional)

Directions

1. Pour half tbsp of coconut oil or maybe butter into a saucepan and place over low heat, add the onions and fry for up to 30 minutes, stirring often until caramelized. When onions seems drying out, sprinkle some water to the pan.

2. Now make the parsnip puree. Slash the parsnips and put into a steamer, steam up to 10 minutes until it's soft enough. Let it cool.

3. After that, get the green beans ready by tidying the ends of green beans and then cut to pieces (about 2 inch). Put the cut green beans into a steamer; steam for 7 minutes or there about until they are soft. When soft enough but not over tender, pour into a baking dish and keep aside.

4. Using the same pan used in frying onions, fry the mushrooms, add more coconut oil or butter if required and place over medium-high heat. Fry for some minutes, add the garlic, and stir until soft. Allow for about 5 minutes to cook. Pour one part of the garlic mushroom mix into the green beans.

5. Now, pour steamed parsnips into a blender, add the remaining half of garlic mushroom, add salt, water and nutritional yeast, and then pulse until smooth. Add pepper and crushed red pepper if you like.

6. Add the mixture to green beans together with mushrooms and stir until mushrooms and green beans are properly coated.

7. Finally, top with the caramelized onions and then bake for half an hour, let it cool, then serve.

Lemon Coconut Lentil Soup

Contents

- 2 tbsp of coconut oil
- 2 stalks of cut celery
- 3 cloves of crushed garlic
- ½ yellow crushed onion
- 1 tsp of smoked paprika
- 1 tsp of cumin
- 2 carrots, chopped
- 4 cups of vegetable broth
- 1/2 cup of tomato paste
- 4 cups of water
- 2 cups of red lentils
- 1/2 tsp of coriander
- 2 tbsp of fresh lemon juice
- 1/3 cup of full-fat coconut milk
- Grounded red pepper flakes
- Sea salt and pepper to taste
- *optional cilantro for garnish (recommended)

Directions

1. In a big pot, dissolve the coconut oil over medium heat, put in your cut onions and let it cook until it becomes clear.
2. Include garlic, carrots, coriander, celery, smoked paprika and cumin and then allow to cook for extra 6 minutes.
3. Put in the broth, lentils, tomato paste and water. Cover the pot, let everything boil together for 28 to 45 minutes, but ensure you lower the heat and cook until lentils becomes soft.
4. Mix in the coconut milk, lemon juice; add pepper and sea salt to season.
5. Use grounded red pepper flakes, fresh cilantro and lemon wedge to top when serving.

Balsamic Kale & Chicken Sausage Dessert

Contents

For the crust
- 3 cups of unbleached general flour
- 1 cup of hot water (120o F)
- ½ tsp of dried oregano
- 1½ tsp of sugar
- 1½ tsp of active dry yeast
- ½ tsp of salt
- ½ cup of chickpeas, washed and drained
- 1½ tsp of dry ranch dressing mix
- 1 tsp of basil

For the dessert
- 1 cup of sliced de-stemmed kale
- 1 tsp of coconut oil
- 2 cups of chopped mozzarella cheese
- 1 tsp of balsamic vinegar
- 2 chicken sausages, chopped
- 1 tsp of basil cream or alternatively 6 fresh basil leaves
- 1 cup of dessert sauce

Directions

1. Mix into the hot water in a bowl, sugar and active dry yeast. Allow the mixture stay for about 14 to 17 minutes for the yeast to actuate and turn foamy.

2. Mix in the coconut oil and chickpeas into the yeast mixture. Use a blender to puree until smooth. Now add ranch mix, basil, flour, oregano and salt to taste and stir very well. Knead with hands and roll into a ball, then cover with plastic cover and put in the fridge for about 5 hours before baking

3. Sprinkle the baking tray with nonstick oil. Preheat oven to 425o F.

4. Revolve the dough and place onto a floured sheet and knead for some time. Flatten the dough with a rolling pin to roughly 13inch wide and about ½ inch thick. Move onto the already arranged baking sheet and bake for 12 minutes.

5. At this time, melt coconut oil over medium heat, and add in the basil paste, shredded chicken sausage, kale and balsamic vinegar, then allow baking for roughly 5 minutes until sausage is heated and kale is soft.

6. Bring out the incompletely baked dough from oven. Pour the pizza sauce on it, and the cheese, top with chicken sausage and the baked kale. Finally, bake for 10 more minutes or maybe when the cheese dissolves and lightly browned. Cut into chunks and then serve when it's hot.

Maple Banana Bread with Hemp Seeds

Contents

- 3/4 cup of almond flour
- 1/4 cup of tapioca flour
- 1/2 cup of brown rice flour
- 1/2 tsp of baking soda
- 1/2 cup of sorghum flour
- 1 tsp of baking powder
- 1 tsp of sea salt
- 1/4 tsp of grated nutmeg
- 1 tsp of cinnamon
- 1/2 cup of maple syrup
- 1/2 cup of extra virgin coconut oil, melted & cooled
- 2 ripped sizable mashed bananas
- 2 big eggs
- 1 tsp of vanilla extract
- 1/3 cup of almond milk
- 3 tbsp of hemp seeds

Directions

1. Whisk the first nine ingredients in the list above together in a big bowl. Also, in a different bowl, mix together the almond milk, maple syrup, mashed banana, eggs, coconut oil and vanilla until properly mixed.
2. Now, combine the moist ingredients and the dry ingredients by mixing with a spatula until it appears like a heavy cream.
3. Oil your loaf skillet line with paper parchment.
4. Fill the loaf pan with mixture and spread uniformly. Spread hemp seeds on top and bake for about 50 minutes or until toothpick comes out neat without sticky dough.
5. Remove from heat and allow cooling for some minutes and the serve.

Coconut Oil Hollandaise Sauce

Constituents
- 3 tablespoons of coconut oil
- 2 medium egg yolks
- 1 tablespoon of fresh lemon juice
- 1/2 teaspoon salt
- 1/8 teaspoon paprika

Directions
1. Clean up the blender with warm water
2. Let the blender dry totally, next add lemon juice and egg yolks in the blender and blend.
3. The blender running on low, gently add in the warm coconut oil in regular flow.
4. Add salt and paprika, and then blend to mix well.
5. Serve right away over eggs, salmon, asparagus or as sauce for artichokes.

Pumpkin Soufflé

Ingredients

- 1 cup of canned pumpkin puree
- 4 whole eggs
- 1/2 cup of coconut oil, melted
- 2 tablespoons of almond butter
- 5 tsp of maple syrup
- 1 teaspoon vanilla extract
- 1 tsp of coconut flour
- 1/4 teaspoon of baking soda
- 1 teaspoon of cinnamon
- 1/2 teaspoon nutmeg
- 1/2 teaspoon of ground clove
- Small quantity of Sea salt

Process

1. Preheat the oven to 350° F.
2. Whisk together the canned pumpkin, maple syrup, eggs, almond butter, coconut oil until properly mixed.
3. Sift the coconut flour, baking soda, cinnamon, nutmeg and clove into the wet mixture and then keep on mixing until properly mixed.
4. Fill into oven safe ramekins (or souffle dish)
5. Bake in the middle of the oven for 24 to 36 minutes or perhaps until the souffle puffs up while the middle no more looks moist.

Amazing Brownie Bars

Contents

For the brownie layer
- ¼ cup of dissolved coconut oil
- 15 dried medjool pitted dates
- 2 tablespoons of coconut flour
- ¼ teaspoon of baking powder
- 3 whisked eggs
- ¼ cup of unsweetened cocoa powder
- Salt
- 2 spoons of raw honey
- 1 teaspoon of vanilla concentrate
- ¼ teaspoon of baking soda
- salt to taste

For the magic layer
- 2 tablespoons of coconut oil
- 1 1/2 cups of unsweetened chopped coconut
- 1 tablespoon of pure honey
- 2 tablespoons of coconut cream or even homemade coconut butter
- 2 egg whites whisked until frothy

Directions

1. Preheat oven to 365° F.
2. Put the dates into your food processor and beat till it becomes creamy paste.
3. Next, add coconut oil and also cocoa powder into the food processor, and then blend until properly combined smooth.
4. Now, add vanilla, eggs, baking powder, coconut flour, honey, baking soda and salt, keep mixing until smooth.
5. Oil an 8x8 baking pan with some coconut oil and then pour it in the brownie mixture and even out over the pan.
6. Time to add in the coconut oil, chopped coconut, honey and coconut butter into a bowl and heat in the microwave.
7. Mix up all the ingredients together until soft, next add in the whisked egg whites while mixing.
8. Now, pour topping over brownie batter and then even out until everything covers the surface of the brownie.
9. Put in the oven and then bake for 20 to 35 minutes.
10. Allow to cool before you slice into parts. Enjoy!

Fauxtmeal Chocolate Chip Snacks

Ingredients

- 2 cups of white Almond flour
- 1 tbsp of vanilla concentrate
- 1/3 cup of shredded Coconut
- 2 tablespoons of Tapioca flour
- 1/2 cup of melted pure Honey
- 1/3 tsp of baking soda
- 1/4 tsp of sea salt
- 1/2 cup of melted Coconut oil
- 1 tbsp of Gelatin (optional)
- 1/2 cup of chopped chocolate

Instructions

1. Preheat oven to 350o F
2. Mix together, the almond flour, tapioca flour, baking soda, coconut oil, gelatin and the sea salt in a big bowl
3. In another smaller dish, mix the liquid items until properly combined (I heat the pure honey given that it is thick)
4. Now combine the watery mixture into the dry preparation and mix them up until properly mixed.
5. Mix in the chocolate chips
1. Refrigerate for about 20 to 30 minutes to solidify for better feel and scooping
6. Scoop a tablespoon quantity of cookie dough and keep them 2 inches separated on a parchment covered cookie tray
7. Next, you need to press each ball until you achieve the desired thickness since these do not spread (should you want crispy edges, then make sure they are wispy)
8. Position the cookie tray atop another one to avoid the bottoms from browning
9. Put in the oven and bake for 12 to 15 minutes. Keep an eye on them as nobody loves an burnt cookie, you absolutely need them just brown around the bottom sides and then golden on the top
10. Take them out from oven and allow to cool for about 10 minutes before moving to a cooling rack
11. Take with a glass of almond juice or perhaps fresh coconut milk

Cookie Dough Peanuts

Things Needed

- 2 cups of white almond flour
- 1/2 cup of tapioca flour or possibly arrowroot starch
- 1/4 tsp salt
- 3 tbsp of natural maple syrup or even honey
- 1 tablespoon of vanilla
- 1 cup of melted coconut oil
- 1/2 Dark chocolate chips and 1 cup of chopped chocolate chips

Directions

1. Dissolve a cup of chocolate chips in microwave and put aside to cool a little.
2. Sift all the dry materials together in a container.
3. Bring in the coconut oil and then mix.
4. Put the maple syrup or just honey, vanilla and chocolate chips.
5. Mix to incorporate well, now roll into balls and place on baking sheet lined with paper parchment
6. Put into a refrigerator for 12 to 16 minutes.
7. Next, remove from refrigerator and immerse in melted chocolate, then put in back to refrigerator for 22 to 35 minutes until the chocolate is solidified.
8. Remove from fridge and Eat.

Remark: You will get perfect result when kept in a refrigerator which enables it to last several days in case they're not finished immediately.

Thin Mints

Formula

For the cookie:
- 1/2 cup of tapioca starch
- 1 oz of melted chocolate
- 1/4 tsp salt
- 1/4 tsp of baking soda
- 1 tsp vanilla concentrate
- 1/2 cup coconut flour
- 1 cup of natural coconut oil
- 2 tbsp of natural cocoa powder powder
- 1 egg
- 1/4 cup of natural maple syrup

For the chocolate covering
- 2 tbsp of coconut oil
- 1 tbsp of natural peppermint concentrate
- 2 cups of chocolate

Instructions

For the cookie:

1. Mix all these together in a medium sized bowl - tapioca starch, baking soda, cocoa powder, coconut flour and pinch of salt

2. Mix the coconut oil, vanilla, maple syrup and egg in a mixer.

3. Melt the chocolate, pour into the soggy preparation. Stir until well mixed.

4. With the mixing machine running on low, now bring in 50% of the dry mixture and stir until properly integrated. Don't forget to abrade the sides. Next, bring in the last part of the dry mixture and continue to stir until well combined.

5. Use scooper to scoop dough on a sheet of plastic wrap. Finish off and then put into refrigerator for about an hour.

6. Now remove dough from refrigerator and place on desk for just a few minutes. Preheat oven to 350o F.

7. Set the dough ball on a sil-pat, position a section of plastic cover over the top and then utilize a rolling pin to roll out, about 1/4 inch thick.

8. When you finish the roll out, set the sil-pat on a baking sheet, place in the refrigerator for about five minutes and remove, then use one small cookie cutter to form circles at the center. Using a spatula, pick and set them on a covered baking tray. Finish off. (The dough should be hard to pick them up and set on baking tray, hence don't forget to refrigerate).

9. Bake for 10 to 15 minutes, remove from oven and allow for about 10 minutes to cool on a rack.

For chocolate covering:

1. Melt the chocolate.
2. Mix together the coconut oil and peppermint concentrate until fully combined.
3. Now dip every cookie in the melted chocolate and shake off excess chocolate.
4. Set on a parchment lined baking tray and then put into the freezer for about 6 minutes
5. When it's hard, remove from freezer and eat! (Keep the rest in a freezer).

Matcha and Coconut Chubby Bombs

Contents

For the cookies
- 1 cup of greasy coconut butter (or try homemade)
- 1 cup of solid coconut oil (refrigerate if need be)
- 1 tsp of natural vanilla concentrate (you can make yours)
- 1/2 tsp matcha green tea powder
- 1 cup of whole fat coconut milk (refrigerate overnight)
- ¼ tsp of ground Ceylon cinnamon
- ½ tsp Himalayan salt

For the layering
- 1 tbsp of matcha green tea powder
- 1 cup of thinly cut unsweetened coconut

Direction

1. In a big sized mixing bowl, combine all the first items under cookies. Remember that the coconut oil must be solid, very necessary thus to achieve that you can put in a freezer for some time. Also, refrigerate the coconut milk. Although, you really may not use the cream portion only, however you're free to use only that should you like to.

2. With a hand mixer, blend on high speed the items until soft and crispy, after that put in the fridge for like one hour to solidify.

3. As the "truffle" blend is in the fridge to solidify, next mix the nicely cut coconut together with matcha powder in medium sized mixing bowl and keep aside.

4. Using a small ice-cream scooper, scoop the cold solid truffle mixture into little balls, more or less like the size of ping pong ball.

5. Shape the balls into nice spheres by rolling between your palms, next dip the spheres into the coconut-matcha mixture and then roll until fully covered with coconut-matcha mixture.

6. Next, move the completed fat bombs into an airtight container and then refrigerate for about two weeks.

7. Remove and Enjoy. You can eat them straight from fridge however they are much better if you allow them to stay for 12 to 17 minutes at room temperature before eating them.

Chocolate Dark Cherry Tart

To make a small tart (7" skillet), however you can increase this treat for a complete size tart skillet.

Crust Formula
- 1/2 cup of coconut flour
- 1/2 tbsp of natural vanilla concentrate
- 1/3 cup of liquid sweetener that you like
- 1/2 cup of cocoa powder
- 1/2 cup of apple butter (apple sauce would do the trick as well)
- 1/4 tsp of salt
- 1 cup of water
- 1/2 cup of melted coconut oil
- 1/2 cup of tapioca starch

Filling Materials
- 1 cup of coconut oil
- 2 tsp of natural vanilla concentrate
- 1 cup of cocoa powder
- 2 cups of cherries, pitted and halved
- 5 tbsp of liquid sweetener of your choosing (or maple syrup)
- Salt to taste

For Topping
- Chocolate nibs and additional cherries for garnish

Instructions

1. Preheat oven to 350° F.
2. Lubricate your tart skillet and keep it aside.
3. In a big mixing bowl, combine all crust materials together, apart from cocoa powder, tapioca starch and coconut flour. Using an immersion mixer, blend all the items until soft and frosty. Please, in case you don't have immersion blender, then, this can be done using your food processor or even your hand. Now, bring in leftover crust items and combine the mixture using your hand, kneading it gently until it becomes gummy smooth dough.
4. Next, pour the dough into the tart skillet, press it and widen uniformly in the skillet (with your fingers until it takes the tart pan. You can use fork to make holes on the base of the crust to reduce bubbling when baking. Put in the oven and allow baking for about 25 minutes. Take them out from oven, place on a rack to cool.
5. Spread the cut cherries evenly on the tart base and put it aside.
6. Now put together the chocolate filling, Put the chocolate filling over cherries on the tart.
7. Put the tart in the refrigerator for like one hour to let the chocolate filling solidify.
8. Next, the moment it's set then spread the chocolate nibs and embellish with additional cherries.
9. Remove from refrigerator and keep at room for that creamy and gel-like texture or serve immediately.
10. Enjoy!

Note: To keep the chocolate filling hard, then keep refrigerated.

Lemon Opiate Paleo Muffins

Constituents

- Lemon Zest
- 3 tbsp of lemon juice
- 1 tsp of vanilla concentrate
- 4 eggs
- ¼ cup of ghee or coconut oil, melted
- ¼ cup of honey
- 1 tbsp of Opiate seeds
- ½ teaspoon of baking soda
- ⅛ teaspoon salt
- ⅓ cup of coconut flour

Directions

1. Preheat oven to 350 o F. Oil or simply line muffin tin with parchment.
2. Combine all of the materials together apart from poppy or opiate seeds in a food processor and blend until properly mixed. Now, add in the poppy seeds and blend
3. Put in the oven and bake for about 23 to 35 mins or until golden brown, you can check by using toothpick to insert in the middle and if it comes clean when pulled out. Place on a wire rack and allow to cool.

Strawberry Mousse

Components
- 1 cup of melted coconut oil
- 2 oz of Parched Strawberries
- 1 average sized avocado
- 1 tsp of vanilla
- 2 big sized ripened bananas
- ¼ tsp of sea salt
- 15 freshly ripened strawberries
- 1 tbsp of maple syrup

Directions
1. Put all of the items in a food processor and then pulse until silky.
2. Then let it cool for 60 minute.
3. Consume!

Natural Sweet Potato Salad with Curry Almond Sauce

Materials
- 2 big sweet potatoes
- 1 cup of sliced walnuts
- ½ cup of melted coconut oil
- 1 cup of dried currants

For Curry Almond Sauce
- 6 tsp of curry powder
- 2 tbsp of tamari
- ½ cup of almond butter
- 2 tsp of cinnamon
- 2 tbsp of apple cider vinegar

Instructions
1. Blend all the Curry Almond Sauce items together
2. Now skin the sweet potatoes and use peeler to prepare raw sweet potato noodles or grate just grate them.
3. Next in a bowl, mix the sweet potato noodles, the walnuts and currants together and then apply the sauce into the sweet potato salad.

Rosemary with Sea Salt Crackers

Constituents
- 2 cups of almond flour
- 1 tbsp of nicely cut rosemary
- 1/4 tsp Celtic sea salt
- 1 egg
- 1/4 tsp of black pepper
- 2 tbsp of coconut oil

Guidelines
1. Preheat oven to 350° F
1. Mix almond flour with the sea salt in a big bowl.
2. Now, mix together a different bowl the rosemary, coconut oil, black pepper and egg.
3. Add the two mixtures together and stir very well to combine
4. Roll the dough between 2 items of parchment paper until roughly 1/4" thick
5. Slice the dough just straight strips and also cut in sideway strips. (you can cut the dough with pizza cutter. This makes as much as 36 crackers).
6. Set the fragments on a baking sheet lined with parchment and then bake in the oven for about 12 to 18 or perhaps until it turns golden brown.

Natural Walnut Fudge

Constituents

- 1 cup of Walnut Pulp (remaining from preparing a portion walnut milk)
- Otherwise 1 cup of fresh Walnut
- 1 cup of melted coconut oil
- Sea salt to taste
- 1 cup of fresh cocoa powder
- 1 cup of maple syrup
- 2 tsp of vanilla
- 1 tbsp of walnut oil, virgin olive oil or pumpkin seed oil (Optional, based on the flavor you really want to achieve.)
- GARNISH: ½ cup of coarse sliced fresh walnuts

Directions

1. When using remaining walnut pulp, then stay on the instructions right here to make a fresh gallon of walnut milk. (Simply immerse the walnuts for like 2 hours, then wash and blend with four cups of water. Press with nut milk bag in addition, preserve the remaining walnut fiber pulp for the preparation of this fudge)

2. Now in a food processor, mix together the walnut pulp powdered cocoa maple syrup, walnut oil, melted coconut oil, vanilla and season with sea salt (mainly all the ingredients but the 3/4 cup of walnuts reserved for garnishing).

3. Using saran wrap or parchment to line a not so big square dish like Tupperware square dish, about 4 by 5 inches.

4. Scoop the fudge mixture into these square dishes.

5. Spread the sliced walnuts on top, moving some in and put the final coating.

6. Put in the freezer for about 60 minutes or longer.

7. Cut into squares, Serve and enjoy. Tastes great when refrigerated

Attention: The quantity left over of walnut pulp you obtain is based on how long they're soaked in water before milk. In the event you didn't first soak them, there will be more leftover pulp compared to when you soak for several hours. This is because soaking really helps to break down the nut, in addition to eliminating bitterness from the tannins.

Toffee Bars

Contents
- 2 cups of unsweetened sliced coconut
- 1 tsp of vanilla concentrate
- 1 cup of melted coconut oil
- 2 eggs
- 2/3 cup of coconut sugar
- ¼ tsp of salt
- 1 cup of chocolate chips

Directions
1. Preheat oven to 350° F.
2. With parchment line 9 by 13 inch baking container.
3. Now, combine the eggs, coconut sugar, vanilla, unsweetened chopped coconut, salt and coconut oil together.
4. Spread evenly into baking dish.
5. Put into oven and bake for about 24 to 35 minutes, or until mildly browned.
6. Remove container and then spray with cacao chips. Put into oven again for some minutes so as to let the chocolate chips dissolve, distribute the melted chips with spatula.
7. Let it cool for chocolate to harden again.
8. Now, cut into squares.
9. Serve right away or perhaps place in freezer.

Chocolate Block Cookie Bars

Contents
- 1 cups of high-quality almond flour
- ½ cup of coconut sugar
- ¼ Teaspoon of sea salt
- 1 tsp of baking powder
- 1 tsp of tapioca starch
- 2/3 cup (or 3 ounces) of chocolate chunks,
- ⅓ cup of melted coconut oil.
- 1 egg
- 1 tbsp of vanilla concentrate

Directions
1. Preheat the oven to 350°F gently oil a baking skillet about 11 by 7" in size.
2. In a sauce pan, dissolve the coconut oil on low heat.
3. In a bowl, mix the baking powder, almond flour, sea salt, tapioca starch and coconut sugar together.
4. Dice the chocolate bars and mix them up into the almond flour preparation.
5. Now, add the melted coconut oil, vanilla and egg, and continue mixing to form smooth cookie dough
6. Spread out the cookie dough evenly on the prepared pan. Never fret in case the dough is hard and rough, it would make a good crunchy after baking.
7. Put in the oven and bake for about 13 to 17 minutes or perhaps, until the cookie bars are golden brown but still clammy in the middle.

Vanilla Toasted Coconut and Cashew Shake

Contents
- 350g of unsweetened flaked coconut
- 2 tbsp of melted coconut oil
- 350g of fresh unsalted natural cashews
- ¼ teaspoon of sea salt
- 1 tbsp of pure vanilla juice

Directions
1. Preheat oven to 325° F.
2. Using silpat liner or maybe parchment, line a big baking sheet.
3. Put the coconut & cashews on the baking sheet and then pray vanilla, coconut oil and salt on it. Stir to incorporate fine.
4. Now, spread the mixture evenly then, put in the oven for 17 - 20 minutes to bake until it turns golden brown. Stir every 5 minutes.
5. Remove from oven and allow to completely cool. Put in an airtight jar. You can keep it safe at room temperature.

Tomato Soup

Contents
- 5 sizable cloves garlic
- 2 cups of sliced sweet onion
- 1 cup of coconut oil
- 2 cans of 28oz fire roasted tomatoes
- 2 ½ cups of beef broth
- 1 cup of red wine
- 2 bay leaves
- 1 cup of loosely stuffed torn basil leaves

Process
1. Fry the onions in melted coconut oil for about 15 mins in the oven.
2. Put in the garlic and additionally fry for another 3 mins.
3. Now, pour in the red wine to seethe for more 5 minutes, or till wine sweetness declines.
4. Now, put the beef broth, bay leaves, tomatoes and basil leaves. After that, covered for like 20 minutes and allow to simmer.
5. Remove from heat and let it cool, then take away the bay leaves.
6. Serve and Enjoy!

Parsnip Fries Two-Ways

Contents
- 4 peeled medium parsnips
- 2 or 3 tsp of pumpkin pie spice
- 2 to 3 tsp of hot Hungarian paprika
- 2 tbsp of melted coconut oil, divided
- Sea salt

Directions
1. Preheat oven to 450° F.
2. Line a big baking tray or two small baking trays with parchment
3. Slice parsnips into small bits. Next, split into 2 mixing bowls.
4. Add pumpkin pie spice in one of the bowls, but in the second bowl add in the Hungarian paprika. Sprinkle some sea salt to both bowls.
5. Mix up the spices into the parsnip fries with your hand.
6. Set the mixture on baking tray, and sprinkle one tbsp of melted coconut oil on both sets of bowl.
7. Put in the oven and then bake for 10 to 20 mins on one side, then turn the other side and also allow to bake for 10 to 20 mins.
8. Remove from the oven and then combine the fries together and sprinkle little sea salt when it's still hot.
9. Enjoy.

Lemon Lime Coconut Treats

Contents

- 1 cup of chopped coconut
- 1 cup of coconut butter
- 1 cup of coconut oil
- 2 tbsp of honey or small liquid stevia (optional)
- 1 tsp of vanilla concentrate
- 1 big free natural lemon
- 2 fresh lines
- 1/2 tsp of lemon concentrate
- 1/4 tsp of sea salt

Directions

1. Heat the coconut oil and butter together on low heat to mix up well . If you use sweetener, then bring it in at this point.
2. Now, stir in the chopped coconut including the lime and lemon zest.
3. Bring in the lemon extract, vanilla, salt and lime extract and mix very well.
4. Remove from heat and then add the lime and lemon juice and whisk. The citrus is going to get the coconut cream to curdle for a moment though it'll smooth out back as you continue the mixing.
5. Pour into molds for example, mini silicone muffin skillets or else you may pour it into a glass bowl and cut to chunks afterwards
6. Put in the fridge or freezer to cool and firms.
7. Consume and store the rest in an airtight jar and preserve in the refrigerator.

Sweet Potato Dish With Honey Sweetened Marshmallows

Contents
- 1 portion of Traditional Self-made Marshmallows, slice into tiny squares.
- 1/4 cup of butter or cheese, coconut oil
- 5 medium sweet potatoes
- 2 tbsp of honey
- 1 tsp of cinnamon
- Rough pepper to taste
- 1/4 teaspoon nutmeg
- Sea salt

Process

It's better to prepare the marshmallow 4 hours at the least or even a day before the time. Drop these in some arrowroot and then keep in a paper bag or just enclose in cheese material in order to dry up a little.

1. Preheat the oven to 400° F, Wash the sweet potatoes and pat dry.
2. Gently dip each one in butter or maybe and also sprinkle small coarse sea salt. Use fork to thrust holes into each one.
3. Set the sweet potatoes on cookie sheet lined with parchment paper.
4. Put in the oven and bake for like 40 minutes to 60 minutes or rather until soft.
5. Remove from heat and let it cool, after that take off the skin.
6. Now, mix up the sweet potato in a big bowl with the other constituents outlined above and then whisk with a hand mixer until it's smooth.
7. Move to saucepan and bake for approximately 28 to 40 minutes.
8. Take out of oven; allow to cool for 15 minutes. Combine the marshmallows and use a torch like the one used for creme brulée to brown the tops. Serve!

Rosemary Fried Lemons

Ingredients

- 1 cup coconut oil or any other fat you may prefer. (They taste wasn't nice with bacon fat)
- 1 full lemon juice (or meyer)
- 1/4 cup of almond flour
- 1/2 tsp of black pepper
- 1 tbsp of dried rosemary
- 1 egg
- 1/2 tsp of sea salt

For Breakfast time

- 3 eggs
- 3 pieces of bacon

Directions

For Fried Lemons

1. Pour your oil into a small saucepan that's deep and heat over medium heat.
2. Beat one egg in a small bowl and keep.
3. Combine together in another bowl, the almond flour, pepper, salt and rosemary and stir
4. Cut the lemon with sharp knife 1/7 inch thick.
5. Dip the lemon in the egg, clean and layer each side with the almond flour mixture and put aside
6. Heat the oil, you may test it by dipping a spoon in the oil and if it boils, that means it's hot.
7. Put in the sliced lemons in the oil, allow to fry for about 1 minute then turn the other sides of the lemon and allow to simmer for another 30 seconds. Now, remove all of them from oil. (Be watchful lest they burn).
8. Place fried lemons on paper towel to cool. Then serve right away.

For Morning meal

1. Cook your bacon using a cookie sheet lined with an aluminum foil in the oven at 375o F.
2. Turn the bacon, let continue cooking for extra 15 minutes till it's crunchy.
3. Now cook 3 sides up eggs, spray it with pepper and rosemary and then heat over medium heat.
4. Remove from heat and serve with the lemons.

Chocolate Chip Blondies

Contents
- 2 cups of almond flour
- 1/2 cup of coconut flour (recommended Tropical Traditions or even Bob's Red Mill)
- 1 cup of unsweetened cut coconut (TT or maybe BRM)
- 1 1/2 tsp of baking powder
- 1 tsp of baking soda
- 1/8 tsp of Himalayan salt
- 1 tsp of pure Trader Joe's Stevia, otherwise any sweetener out there can do.
- 1 tbsp of natural honey (optional)
- 1 cup of sliced nuts (walnuts or pecans)
- 1/2 cup of chocolate chips
- 3 sizable eggs
- less than 1/2 cup of melted virgin coconut oil or simply any unsalted butter
- 2 tsp of natural vanilla extract

For Topping
- 2 tbsp of cut nuts
- 2 tbsp of chocolate chips

Directions

1. Preheat oven to 325° F.
2. Oil an 8 by 8" saucepan with coconut oil but line the base with parchment.
3. Mix the dry contents together in a medium sized bowl
4. Put in the leftover constituents and stir with a wooden spoon. Taste for sweetness, adjust if necessary. Distribute the mixture into pan and apply further chocolate nut and chips on top of the mixture and bake in the oven for about 25 minutes. According to how clammy you may prefer your own brownies.
5. Serve when still warm or even serve with Vanilla Bean Gelato at room temperature
1. In the event you do not have chopped coconut, then use food processor to blend coconut chips or flaked one to make the smaller.

Reese's Swirl Brownies

Contents:

- 3 ounce of dark chocolate bar, 60% or more of cacao (Alter Eco recommended)
- 3/4 cup of soft Barney Butter or even sun butter, divided into 1/4 cup and 1/2 cup
- 1 cup of melted coconut oil.
- 1/2 cup of grade b natural maple syrup,
- 3 raw eggs (cage free)
- 1/4 teaspoon vanilla
- 2/3 cup of coconut sugar
- 1 cup healthy chocolate chips
- 1/2 cup of unsweetened cacao powder

Instructions

1. Preheat oven to 350o F.
2. Using double boiler, melt the dark chocolate bar by putting the metal bowl dark chocolate bar in another pot of boiling water.
3. Remove the chocolate from heat when it dissolves and then stir in gently the liquid coconut oil.
4. Now add the 1/4 cup of almond butter (or alternatively sunflower seed butter for nut-free treat), vanilla extract, eggs and maple syrup.
5. Combine the dry contents the coconut palm sugar as well as the unsweetened cocoa powder
6. Flip in the chocolate chips.
7. Pour the brownie mixture into an 8 by 8 inches square glass skillet oiled with coconut oil or even butter. Now, evenly spread the leftover 1/2 cup of almond butter on top of mixture, then carefully glide a butter knife about to make whirls on the batter.
8. Cook it for like 30 minutes or more, or if toothpick comes out neat, then remove from heat and allow to cool. Enjoy your meal.

Mammoth Chocolate Chip Pumpkin Snacks

Contents

- 1 cup of pumpkin puree
- 1 cup of coconut oil
- 1/3 cup of arrowroot powder
- 2 eggs
- ½ cup of coconut sugar
- 1/3 cup of coconut flour
- 2 tsp of vanilla extract
- 2/3 cup of mini chocolate chips
- 1 tsp of cinnamon
- ½ tsp of baking soda
- 1 tsp of pumpkin pie spice
- ½ tsp of sea salt

Directions

1. Preheat oven to 350o F. Mix all these together in a bowl, coconut flour, baking soda, pumpkin pie spice, sea salt, arrowroot and cinnamon and reserve. .

2. Now, properly blend coconut oil and coconut sugar together with a mixer until it turns creamy.

3. Bring in the eggs and vanilla and continue mixing, add pumpkin puree.

4. Now, gradually incorporate the flour mixture and then mix to properly combine together. Also put in the chocolate chips.

5. When properly mixed, use a small batter cup like 1/4 to create about 3" cookies on baking sheet lined with parchment.

6. Put in the oven and bake for about 13 to 17 minutes, remove from oven and then move to wire rack to cool. You can store your cookies in the fridge. Enjoy!

Tip: In case you are unable to get the batter into a big cookie, then you will have to use more coconut flour to thicken it.

Sweet Potato Cookies

Contents:

- 1/4 cup of tapioca flour
- 3/4 cup of almond flour (or sunflower seed flour for nut-free)
- 1/3 cup of coconut flour
- 1 tbsp of baking powder (sodium)
- 1/2 tsp of sea salt
- 1/4 cup of coconut oil, solid (or alternatively butter or even palm shortening)
- 1 modest sweet potato, baked and also mashed (about 88 grams)
- 1/2 cup or higher of light coconut milk
- Seasonings to taste (nutmeg, onion powder, cinnamon, ginger, and garlic powder)

Instructions
1. Preheat oven to 425° F.
2. Line your baking sheet with parchment paper.
3. Now mix the first four dried contents in a mixing bowl, add salt and seasonings (optional) to taste
4. Gently mix in the coconut oil. After mixing in the coconut oil you need to press the batter together into big crumbs.
5. Now, mash in the sweet potato until thoroughly mixed.
6. Finally, add the 1/2 cup of coconut milk and also mix properly. You can add more as required and then allow it to sit for 5 minutes to let the coconut flour absorb the liquids.
7. You can use tablespoon to scoop the dough onto baking tray lined with parchment paper and for more uniform shape, you can roll them with your hands. Then, use your fingers to slightly press on the balls to flatten them.
8. Put in the oven and bake for about 18 - 20 minutes, moreover, constantly check it. You will notice that the edges will start changing color to dark golden brown, once well baked, take out of oven and let them cool, but when you slice into the cookies and you notice there's slight wet inside, then put back in the oven and bake for some more minutes to get dried.
9. Eat and Enjoy.

Almond Flour Bread Meal

Contents
- 1.1/2 cups of Almond Flour
- 1 cup of Coconut Flour
- 1/4 cup of Ground Chia Seeds or Flaxseeds
- 4 Eggs
- 1 tbsp of Apple Cider Vinegar
- 5 tbsp of Melted Coconut oil
- 1/2 Teaspoon of baking soda
- 1/4 tsp of sea salt

Directions
1. Mix all dry contents together in a mixing container and also mix all wet contents together in a different bowl.
2. Incorporate the two mixtures - the dry and wet mixtures.
3. When properly mixed, then pour into 7.5 by 3.5 inch loaf skillet and smooth the top.
4. Put in the preheated oven and bake for about 45 to 60 minutes.
5. After baking, allow it to cool and then slice.
6. Enjoy!
7. (Note: This recipe only makes one small loaf of bread, but if you want to get more loafs then, you should increase the quantity)

Maple Plantain Dessert

Contents

- 1/2 cup of coconut flour, sifted
- 1/2 cup of virgin coconut oil
- 4 eggs
- 1/4 cup of maple syrup
- 2 tsp of cream of tartar
- 1/4 tsp of salt
- 1 cup of ripened plantain, mashed (1 big plantain)
- 4 tsp of vanilla concentrate
- 1/2 tsp of baking soda

Directions

1. Preheat oven to 350o F. Mix the cream of tartar together with the egg whites in a dish bowl.
2. Beat the egg whites until it forms stiff peaks
3. Blend together the maple syrup and coconut oil in a different bowl.
4. It's time to add in egg yolks and continue blending until smooth, stir in the mashed plantain as well as vanilla until properly combined.
5. Now, incorporate the sifted coconut flour, salt and baking soda, mix till it becomes smooth. Gradually mix the egg yolk mixture together with the beaten egg white into the batter.
6. Oil the sides of your cake pan but line the base with parchment and pour the batter into it.
7. Put in the oven and bake for about 30 to 40 minutes, or until top turns light brown and a toothpick come out clean.
8. Enjoy! Note: if you didn't consume everything, then you can cut and refrigerate.

Pumpkin Spice Granola Crunch

Contents
- 1 cup of walnuts or else pecans (soaked, dry roasted)
- 1 cup of almonds (soaked, dry roasted)
- 1/4 cup of ground golden flaxseed
- 1 cup of pumpkin seeds (soaked, dry roasted)
- 5 tbsp of pumpkin puree
- 2 tsp of cinnamon
- 1/2 tsp of nutmeg
- Ground ginger
- 1 tsp of maple extract
- 4 tbsp of coconut oil
- 2 tbsp of maple syrup

Directions
1. Preheat oven to 300o F. Line your baking tray with parchment paper.
2. Nicely chop the walnuts or pecans and the almonds using nut chopper.
3. Mix all the other contents in a bowl
4. Scoop granola onto a baking tray and evenly spread
5. Bake for about 15 minutes, turn and continue for extra 10 to 20 minutes.
6. Granola is usually golden brown when well prepared.
7. Let it cool thoroughly before savoring.
8. You can serve it with coconut milk, yogurt or fresh cream.

Raspberry Coconut Scones

Contents

- 3 cups of almond flour
- $^{1}/2$ cup of golden flax seed meal
- 3/4 cup of chopped coconut (unsweetened)
- ½ cup of grainy erythritol or maybe any preferable sweetener
- 1 tbsp of baking powder
- ¼ tsp salt
- 2 big eggs, moderately beaten
- 2/3 cup of dissolved coconut oil
- 1/2 cup of almond milk
- 3/4tsp of coconut or else vanilla concentrate
- 1 cup of iced up raspberries

Instruction

1. Preheat oven to 325o F.
2. In Mix together in a big mixing bowl, the almond flour, chopped coconut, flax seed flour, baking powder, salt and erythritol sweetener.
3. Now, mix in your eggs, almond milk, coconut oil, vanilla concentrate or coconut. It would be quite gooey.
4. Combine the raspberries and mix until evenly distributed.
5. Pour dough on lined cookie skillet, spread and pat it to rectangle, cut into even portions, again diagonally cut each portion in half to form triangular scones.
6. Carefully distance each cone on cookie tray and space them about 1 inch apart. Put in the oven and bake for 30 to 35 minutes or perhaps until firm when touched and golden brown.
7. Remove from oven and allow to cool on the skillet.

Coconut Raspberry Chocolate Chip Muffins

Muffins are ideal, fast and simple breakfast time meals, most importantly with young children in your house. Coconut flour-based cacao chip muffins are sources of decent nourishment; moreover, they're nice treats. When combined with freeze dried berries, because fresh berries have a tendency of adding much wetness that makes the muffins very clammy.

Contents

- 1 cup of coconut flour
- 1/2 cup of sweetener or maybe any other erythritol
- 3/4 cup of unsweetened chopped coconut
- 1/4 tsp salt
- 1/2 cup of dissolved Kelapo coconut (or perhaps any other good coconut oil)
- 1 tbsp of baking powder
- 3 ounces of dark chocolate bar
- 5 sizable eggs
- 1 tsp of vanilla concentrate
- 3/4 cup of almond milk or simply water
- 1 cup of freeze dehydrated raspberries

Instruction

1. Preheat oven to 350o F. Line your muffin pan with parchment
2. Mix the coconut flour, sweetener, chopped coconut, salt and baking powder together in a big mixing bowl.
3. Now, gradually bring in the coconut oil, vanilla concentrate, chocolate chips, eggs and almond milk and stir very well until properly mixed.
4. Put the mixture into the lined muffin containers and then bake for about twenty minutes or until slightly browned and also firm when touched. Take away from heat and allow for about 15 minutes cooling, and then serving.

Chocolate Chip Mini Muffins

Contents
- 1 cup of almond flour
- 1/2 teaspoon of baking soda
- Dash of sea salt
- 1 natural egg or just 1 flax egg
- 2 tbsp of melted butter or pure coconut oil
- 2 tbsp of pure natural honey (or just maple syrup)
- 2/3 tsp of vanilla concentrate
- 2 tbsp of cacao chips

Instructions
1. Preheat oven to 350°F.
2. Set a rack at the center.
3. Now liberally oil some small muffin tin and keep.
4. Mix together in a bowl the almond flour, salt, baking soda, gently stir in the egg, vanilla, honey and butter, and mix until properly combined. Tuck in small chocolate chips.
5. Scoop the mixture to fill up each small muffin cans.
6. It should yield about a dozen muffins.
7. Put in the oven and bake for like 9 to 10 minutes or until a toothpick comes clear.
8. Place on a rack and allow cooling for some time.

Natural Blueberry Orange Scones

Contents

- 1 cup of coconut flour
- 1 cup of almond flour
- 1 cup of cashew flour
- 1 tbsp of coconut oil
- 1 1/2 cup of almond milk (or whole milk)
- 2 tsp of baking powder
- Dash of salt
- 1/4 cup of coconut sugar (or use natural cane sugar)
- Zest of 1 orange
- 1/2 cup of frozen natural blueberries

Instructions

1. Preheat oven to 400° F. Now line your baking tray with parchment paper
2. In a big mixing bowl, mix all the flours together, as well as salt and baking powder
3. Add in the thick coconut oil using fork or spoon and mix it into the flours until it's uniform and friable.
4. Bring in the orange zest and sugar, mix to combine.
5. Pour in the milk and then stir with a spatula.
6. Fold in the blueberries until properly all over the dough.
7. Move the dough to baking sheet, with hands, make into a circular form.
8. Spread on top with natural cane sugar, with your hands, slightly press into the dough. (This is optional)
9. Cut the dough into 8 even parts and then bake for 17 to 25 minutes until the sides are crunchy and light brown.
10. Now, remove from the oven, allow on the baking sheet to cool for about ten minutes.
11. With a spatula yank the m apart then serve.

Coconutty Granola

Contents
- 1 pound of fresh cashews roughly cut
- 1/2 cup of almond flour
- 8 ounces of fresh cut almonds
- 4 ounces of fresh hazelnuts, roughly cut
- 2 ounces of sesame seeds
- 1/2 cup of ground flaxseed flour (either brown or golden colour)
- 1/2 cup of coconut palm sugar
- 1 tsp of ground cinnamon
- 1 teaspoon of sea salt
- Little ground nutmeg
- 8 ounces of sweetened, shaved coconut flakes
- 2/3 cup of melted pure, virgin coconut oil
- 1/2 cup of pure maple syrup
- 1 teaspoon of natural vanilla extract
- 1/4 teaspoon almond extract

Directions

1. Preheat oven to 325° F, position the oven racks to 2nd and 4th steps from top.

2. Assuming you have a food processor (Otherwise use your hand to cut). With food processor beat the hazelnuts as well as cashew nuts into little pieces, be careful not to over beat to powder. Now, mix up the nuts with other dry contents (The chopped almonds, almond or flax flour, cinnamon, salt, coconut, palm sugar, sesame seeds and the nutmeg) until properly mixed.

3. Use a measuring cup to measure out 2/3 cup of dissolved coconut oil together with 1/3 cup of maple syrup Stir in the almond and vanilla extracts to the measuring cup and then mix the up. Now, spread this liquid blend on the dry mixture and mix to evenly distribute. It is perfect to mix with a washed hand to achieve good mixture.

4. Evenly distribute the granola on your baking tray to have even layer.

5. Put them in the oven, bake for about 15 minutes undisturbed.

6. Remove from oven and with a spatula, turn the granola around and spread again to one layer. Then put back into the oven and then allow baking for extra 15 minutes.

7. Take out and let your granola completely cool before serving. Keep the left over in an airtight glass jar. Enjoy!

Donuts with Coconut Flour

Contents

For Donuts
- 1/2 cup of Coconut flour
- 1/4 cup of lightly toasted chopped coconut
- 1 tsp of baking powder
- 1/2 cup of unsweetened almond milk
- 1/4 tsp salt
- Coconut or your preferred oil for donuts frying
- 1/4 cup of dissolved coconut oil
- 1/4 cup of erythritol or any other sweetener
- 4 sizable eggs
- 1/2 tsp vanilla
- 1/4 tsp stevia

For Outside layer:
- 1/4 cup of sweetener or even any powdered erythritol

Directions

1. Preheat oven to 325° F.
2. Mix the coconut flour, baking powder, salt and sweetener together in a big mixing bowl.
3. Mix in almond milk, eggs, vanilla, coconut oil and stevia, mix properly until the mixture is smooth.
4. Prepare donuts in wells in donut pan, just 2/3 full and bake until all is baked
5. Bake for 16 minutes, or simply until well ready and slightly turns brown by the sides. Take out of oven and allow for 5 minutes in the pan to cool, turn them out onto a wire rack to completely cool.
6. Now pour oil about $^1/2$ inch deep into a big frying pan and heat over medium heat.
7. Now mix the toasted coconut together with powdered sweetener in a mixing food bowl.
8. Now that the oil is sizzling, put in donuts in the oil to fry. Turn the opposite side after some moments as they brown rapidly. Remove them from hot oil and immediately immerse both sides in the coconut to cover the outer layers gently depressing to stick on.
9. Allow to cool on wire rack and serve warm. Enjoy!

Pumpkin Coconut Flour Pancakes

Contents

- 1/2 cup of coconut flour
- 1 tsp of baking powder
- 1/4 cup of vanilla hemp protein powder (or just whey protein powder)
- 1/4 cup of swerve sweetener (or just honey or maple syrup for a paleo type)
- 3 tbsp of melted Kelapo coconut oil
- 1 tsp of cinnamon
- 1/4 tsp of cloves
- 1/2 tsp of salt
- 6 large of eggs
- 1/2 tsp of ginger
- 1/2 cup of pumpkin puree
- 1/2 tsp of vanilla extract
- 1/2 cup of unsweetened coconut milk or maybe almond milk
- Coconut oil for the pan

Directions

1. Preheat oven to 200F.
2. Beat, coconut flour, baking powder, protein powder, cinnamon, ginger, cloves, sweetener and salt together in a big mixing bowl.
3. Mix pumpkin puree, 1/2 cup of almond milk, eggs, vanilla extract and dissolved coconut oil together in another bowl.
4. Now, combine the egg mixture and the coconut flour mixture together and then mix properly to combine. You can add more almond milk in case mixture is thick moreover, it must not be too wet.
5. Place a big pan on medium to high heat, pour some coconut oil. Now that the oil is heated, scoop the mixture into the pan and spread. Perform this until you finish the pancake.
6. Prepare until base is golden brown while the top is set around the sides. Carefully turn as you as it's still on fire until both sides have become golden brown. Gently remove from skillet and allow to cool. Enjoy.

Vanilla-Scented Baked Cashew/Coconut Blend

Contents
- 350g of unsweetened flaked coconut
- 350g natural unsalted cashews
- 2 tbsp of deissolved coconut oil
- 1 tbsp of natural vanilla extract
- ½ teaspoon of sea salt (to taste)

Directions
1. Preheat oven to 325o F. line a big baking tray with parchment.
2. Put the cashews and flaked coconut on baking tray sprinkle with salt, vanilla and coconut oil. Stir with spatula to mix properly.
3. Widen the combination out in a uniform layer, bake for about 17 to 25 minutes until sweet-smelling and mild golden while turning the mixture at 2 minutes interval.
4. Remove from heat and let it cool completely, Server. Move the leftover to an airtight jar and keep at room temperature.

Roasted Brussels Sprout Chips

Contents
- 1 reasonable circular container of cut Brussels sprouts
- 2 garlic cloves, ground
- 2 tbsp of extra-virgin olive oil
- 2 tbsp of melted coconut oil
- 1/2 teaspoon salt
- ½ teaspoon recently ground black pepper

Instructions
1. Preheat oven to 425° F. You need to line baking tray with parchment or maybe aluminum foil.
2. Cut the Brussels sprouts into ⅛" pieces, except outmost leaves.
3. Mix Brussels sprout pieces as well as outmost leaves with garlic, coconut oil and olive oil. Spice up with pepper and salt.
4. Distribute sliced Brussels sprout and leaves in one layer on the lined baking sheet and bake for about 17 minutes for the leaves becomes soft.
5. Remove from heat and server right away.

No-Bake Proteins Bar

This healthy recipe is soy-free, grain-free, egg-free and dairy-free, do-it-yourself protein bar and it's ideal for amazing diets.

Contents

- 2 cups of nuts or seeds, (sunflower, almonds and macadamia or pumpkin. Adding various types of nuts or seed is really great. Preferably, soak the nuts and dry, and use 1⅓ cups of coconut butter)
- 1 cup of flax flour. (Otherwise, utilize rice bran or even protein powder)
- ½ cup of chopped unsweetened coconut
- ½ cup of seed or perhaps nut butter (also prepared from soaked and dried nuts)
- ⅜ teaspoon salt
- ½ cup of coconut oil (or even use cocoa butter)
- 2 tbsp of liquid sweetener - stevia extract
- 2 tsp of vanilla extract

Topping

- Possibly, use Carob Bar or maybe Homemade Chocolate Chips. Use 1 cup of chips for every bar recipe)

Directions

1. Put together the seeds or nuts, coconut, nut or seed butter, salt and flax flour in a food processor and mix.
2. Mix until the seeds or nuts are coarsely ground.
3. Dissolve the coconut oil on low heat.
4. Bring in coconut oil, vanilla and sweeteners into the food processor and mix until properly mixed and it becomes thick paste.
5. Not pour mixture into 8 by 8 square pan.
6. Put into freezer or fridge to chill.
7. As bars are chilling, get the Homemade Carob/Chocolate Bar ready however no need to harden it.
8. Now top bars with the liquid Homemade bar or instead use your own. Return to freezer or fridge to chill.
9. Slice into squares. Serve and Enjoy!
10. Keep leftovers in fridge.

Note

You can use vegetable glycerine for the liquid sweetener for that low carb. However, you can honey or sucanat for even more natural alternatives.

Cauliflower Fried Rice

Contents

- 1 head of natural cauliflower
- 5 cloves of garlic, cleaved
- 2 tbsp of coconut or olive oil
- 8 scallions, slashed (separate white or light green part from dull green tops)
- 2 cups of steamed broccoli, cleaved little
- 1 tsp cleaved natural ginger
- 4 measures of cooked brown rice, chilly
- 1 cup of steamed cut carrots
- 3 tbsp of tamari or diminished sodium soy sauce separated
- 2 eggs, delicately beaten (discretionary for vegetarian)
- 2 tbsp of sesame oil
- 1 lb of your preferred protein (Optional you can use ½ lb pork cut into strips, and also about ¼ lb of shrimps)
- Optional toasted sesame seeds and hacked scallion tops, for enhancement

Directions

1. Take off the cauliflower's hard stems and slash into huge florets.
2. Put cauliflower into a food processor, and blend until it looks like little rice.
3. Heat 1 tbsp of olive oil or coconut oil in a big pan and place on medium heat.
4. Put in the white parts of the ginger, scallions and garlic and cook for about 2 minutes or until the scallions start to mollify.
5. Put in the cauliflower, mix to coat, spread it out in the container, and then let it to cook for few minutes to caramelize.
6. Now Increase heat to medium or high, include the remaining coconut or olive oil and the brown rice, and the turn to coat properly.
7. Spread the blend in the skillet, and allow cooling for 3 minutes to really change the rice to brown.
8. Now, mix in the carrots and broccoli.
9. Make a hole in the middle of rice, and include your proteins as well as 2 tbsp of soy sauce.
10. When the protein is cooked, push to the edges to again make a hole, and pour the eggs, if you're interested in using egg to rapidly scramble.
11. Finally, stir the whole food together and mix in the remaining 2 tbsp of sesame oil and soy sauce.
12. Serve with slashed scallions or with toasted sesame seeds.

Almond - Cheddar Skinned Chicken Chunk

INGREDIENTS

- 1 lb of skinned, boneless Chicken breast – Sliced into small parts
- 1 Big Egg
- 3/4 cup cheddar Cheese – nicely grated
- 1 cup of Almonds
- 1/2 cup thick Cream
- Small Cayenne Pepper
- Coconut oil or Use Olive Oil

Instructions

1. In a food processor, blend the cheese and almonds together to blend very well and grainy.
2. Now, use fort to beat the egg, thick cream and add small dash of cayenne pepper to make wash.
3. Heat some quantity of coconut or olive oil over medium-high heat, it's better to use non-stick pan for your frying. The high corners minimize splash and make cleaning a snap.
4. Cover the chicken parts with your breading and dust in egg wash, after which place one more cover of breading.
5. Time to fry the chicken in the oil, allow cooking very well and the two sides become crispy. You should not turn the chicken parts too often otherwise it may lose your breading
6. You can leave then on a paper bowl or possibly a paper towel which helps to absorb surplus oil.
7. You can opt for any preferred low-carb dipping sauce.
8. SERVE.

Roasted Vegetable & Chorizo Soup

Contents

- 2 cups of cubed rutabaga
- 1 small onion, sliced
- 1 average zucchini, cubed
- 2 average sized eggplant, cubed
- 1 average pepper, sliced
- 1/2 cup of good quality dissolved coconut oil
- 1 tsp of kosher salt
- 1/2 tsp of black pepper
- 6 cups of low sodium chicken broth (do it yourself)
- Pepper and salt to taste
- 12 ounces of chorizo sausage, cut into bit (or any other spicy sausage of choice)

Direction

1. Preheat oven to 450° F.
2. Mix together, the eggplant, onion, rutabaga, zucchini and pepper in a mixing bowl. Now sprinkle with 3 tbsp of melted coconut oil also add the pepper and salt.
3. Bake for about 28 to 30 minutes while stirring vegetables as it cooks.
4. Now heat the leftover 1 tbsp of oil on medium heat using a big saucepan, leave to shimmer however not smoking.
5. Put in the chopped chorizo and cook for 7 to 10 minutes until browned.
6. Now, add in your roasted vegetables together with broth and then allow it to cook.
7. Lower heat to while allowing it to simmer for extra 10 minutes.

Chicken Curry Meal

Contents
- 2 tbsp of Coconut or Olive Oil
- 8 Boneless, Skinned Chicken Thighs (cut into pieces)
- 1 Big Onion, sliced into big chunks
- 3 Small Zucchini, thickly cut
- 1 tsp of diced Garlic
- 1 tbsp of Curry Powder
- 3/4 tsp of Paprika
- 2 tsp of Coarse Original Salt
- 2 Cans (about 15 oz each) of Coconut Milk
- 1 cup of Yellow or Red Grape tomatoes
- Use Cilantro to garnish

Directions
1. Heat olive or coconut oil in a stock pot over high heat. Put in the chicken and then fry until chicken parts turn brown. Take out chicken from the pot and keep aside, leaving the oil in the stock pot.
2. Now, add in zucchini and onion and fry till slightly browned. Include curry powder, salt, garlic and paprika and fry for about 30 seconds more.
3. Pour the chicken into the pot in addition to the coconut milk and allow to cook.
4. Now, reduce heat, cover the pot and allow to simmer for 30 minutes until chicken is properly cooked. Bring in the tomatoes, cook for more 5 minutes. Remove from heat and serve with the coconut broth, just like a soup and you can top it with cilantro.

Coconut-Skinned Mahi Mahi Cookies

Contents
- 1 big egg
- 1 cup of almond flour
- 1 1/4 lb of Mahi Mahi
- 2/3 cup of thinly chopped unsweetened coconut
- 1/4 tsp of pepper
- 1/4 cup of extra virgin coconut oil
- 3/4 tsp of salt
- 4 lime wedges

Guidelines
1. Line cookie sheet with wire cooling rack.
2. Reduce mahi mahi into a couple of inch per piece and with paper towel, pat dry.
3. Whisk egg in big dish. In another big vinyl bowl with a lid, put together the cut coconut, almond flour, pepper and salt, then cover it with the lid and agitate well to mix them up.
4. Put 2 tbsp of the coconut oil in a sizable pan over medium heat. Combine one half leftover of the fish to egg and then stir to coat, but use a grooved spoon or fork to pick objects to the almond flour batter and gently shaking off surplus egg.
5. Set lid on bowl and shake again to coat the fish parts very well. Move fish fragments to skillet and then cook for 3 to 5 minutes per side. Crust usually turns to mild golden brown.
6. Now, pass them onto wire rack to cool even as you finish the rest.
7. Serve and enjoy with lime wedges.

Thai Fish Desserts with Spicy Mayo

Contents

For Fish Desserts
- 3 tbsp of coconut butter
- 2 cloves of garlic
- 1 lb of barramundi filets, skinned and cut into parts
- 3 tbsp of fish sauce (using Red Boat for paleo)
- 2 tbsp of water
- 1 tbsp of grated natural ginger
- 1/2 tsp of chili powder
- 1/2 tsp of red pepper flakes
- 1 tbsp of natural cilantro leaves
- 1/2 tsp of ground cumin
- 2 tbsp of coconut oil
- 1/4 tsp of ground coriander
- Lime wedges
- Spicy Mayo
- 1 1/2 tsp of hot sauce or Sriracha
- 3 tbsp of mayonnaise (using Primal Kitchen for paleo)

Directions

1. To prepare fish cakes or desserts, mix together in a food processor, coconut butter, water, fish, fish sauce, ginger, chili powder, garlic, coriander, cumin, fish sauce and pepper flakes.

2. Beat until the blend turns into a fluffy paste (Always scrape the sides with a spatula).

3. Make into 1 .5 inch balls and then gently press into rissoles of 3/4 inch thick. It is very important to moisten your hands regularly in order not to allow the batter sticking on your hands.

4. Put a big pan over medium heat and add 1 tbsp of coconut oil to dissolve.

5. Now add in just about one half of the fish cakes and be careful to not overcrowd it as you cook for 1 1/2 minutes. Stir and cook for a minute more until properly cooked and turns golden brown.

6. Remove from heat and place on lined plate. Finish off cake.

7. Prepare mayonnaise hot sauce by mixing in a small mixing bowl hot sauce and mayonnaise.

8. Serve desserts hot with a small amount of mayo and lime wedges for garnish

Remarks: Servings may differ based on whether it is for main course or desert.

Coconut Crusted Chicken Rissoles

Contents
- 1 egg yolk
- 1 tsp of onion powder
- 1 pound of quality ground chicken
- 1 cup of unsweetened diced coconut
- 1/4 tsp of garlic powder
- 2/3 tsp of sea salt
- 1 cup of coconut oil
- 1/2 tsp of fresh ground black pepper
- 1/2 tsp of paprika
- 1 cup of almond flour
- Salt and Pepper (as you like)

Directions

1. Preheat oven to 375° F.
2. Add together in a container the almond flour pepper, diced coconut and salt to taste
3. Incorporate to consolidate.
4. Mix together in another mixing bowl, the ground chicken, onion powder, paprika, almond flour, garlic powder, small quantity of sea salt, egg yolk and pepper.
5. Stir to properly mix up all ingredients together.
6. Put coconut oil into a a frying pan and place over medium heat.
7. Now, 2 tablespoons of the chicken mixture, roll into a ball and cover almond-coconut mixture, slightly press flat into the patty. Finish up the remaining. This yields about 12 pieces.
8. Place patties in heated coconut oil; fry each side for 3 minutes. It should be done in small batches.
9. Move fried chicken meatballs onto lined sheet pan and then put in oven for about 5 - 6 minutes to enable chicken to cook properly.

Chocolate Cupcakes with Chocolate Buttercream

Contents

For Cupcake
- 2 cups of general flour
- 2 cups of sugar
- 2 eggs
- 1/2 cup of melted butter
- 2 tsp of vanilla
- 1 cup of cacao powder
- 1 cup of buttermilk
- 1 tsp of baking soda

For Chocolate Frosting
- 1 cup of cacao powder
- 3 1/2 cups of butter, softened
- 2 tsp of vanilla
- burst of salt
- 3 cups of powdered sugar
- 2 tbsp of bulky cream

Directions

1. Preheat oven to 375° F.
2. Line 2 muffin cans with paper parchment, keep aside.
3. Beat sugar and the butter in a big bowl until soft and smooth. Incorporate eggs one after the other and stirring well after each one, then pour vanilla, mix very well.
4. Mix together in a mixing bowl, the flour, baking soda and cocoa powder. Combine with the butter mixture but varying the buttermilk. Stir properly after every addition.
5. Pour into lined muffin cans about 2/3 full and bake for 12 to 17 minutes. Test by inserting toothpick in the middle and if it comes out clean, then remove and allow to completely cool before frosting.
6. Now prepare the frosting, whip the butter in a mid-sized bowl until soft and smooth. Whip in the cacao powder, 1 tbsp of cream, powdered sugar, vanilla and salt. Add extra cream as required. Add frosting as much as you want.

Wholemeal Pasta with Pistachio Pesto

Contents
- 1cup of extra-virgin olive oil
- 2 cups of unsalted roasted shelled pistachios
- 1/2 cup of nicely diced pecorino cheese, reserve extra for serving
- 2 tbsp of sliced mint
- 1 cut garlic clove,
- 2 scallions, cut into 2-inch sizes and garnished
- 1 lb of orecchiette
- Salt

Directions
1. Pulse the pistachios in a food processor, add in garlic, mint and olive oil and continue to blend. Pour the mixture into a bowl and merge in the 1/2 cup of cheese along with the scallions, add salt.
2. Boil your pasta in a big pot of boiling water, add salt and allow cooking until firm and slightly chewy.
3. Drain the water but reserve 1/2 cup of pasta cooking water. Put the pasta in the pot again and then pour in the 1/2 cup of preparation water mix in pesto, cook over low heat. Keep turning until properly coated
4. Remove and serve with cheese.

1 Jalapeno and Ricotta Cauliflower Muffins

Contents
- 2 cups of lightly riced, natural cauliflower
- 1/2 cup of grated parmesan cheese
- 2 eggs, beaten
- 2 tbsp of diced jalapeno
- 2 tbsp of melted butter
- 1 tbsp of dried onion flakes
- 1 cup of grated mozzarella cheese
- 1 cup of grated cheddar cheese
- ½ tsp of garlic powder
- 1/2 tsp of black pepper
- 1 tsp of baking powder
- 1/2 tsp of salt
- 1/2 cup of coconut flour

Directions
1. Mix together in a medium bowl jalapeno, cauliflower, melted butter and eggs; incorporate the grated cheeses and blend well Combine the coconut flour, garlic powder, onion flakes, baking powder, pepper and salt to taste. Blend till completely mixed.
2. Now pour mixture into 12 oiled muffin cups and bake in preheated 375o F oven for half an hour or even until golden brown. Just switch off the oven but leave muffins inside for another one hour to be solid. Take out of oven and then serve.

Chocolate Hardening Sauce

Contents
- 5 tbsp of coconut melted oil
- 1 cup of unsweetened cocoa powder
- 3 tsp of Liquid Stevia and 3 tbsp Swerve Confectioners' sugar free sweetener or Chocolate

Directions
1. Combine all the ingredients together in a mixing bowl and then taste. You can alter sweetener whenever you need more. It will probably not require to be refrigerated

Coconut Almond Fudge

Contents
- 2 tbsp of maple syrup
- 1 cup of almond butter
- ½ tsp of almond extract
- 1 cup of coconut butter
- ¼ tsp of salt
- 1 tbsp of coconut oil

Directions
1. Combine all the contents in a saucepan and mix
2. Heat over medium heat until it is all combined.
3. Put the mixture into molds and keep in a refrigerator to set.

Chocolate Truffles

Contents

- 10 ounces of dark chocolate, 70% or even more of chocolate content
- 1 cup of full-fat coconut milk
- 1 tsp of vanilla concentrate
- 3 tbsp of coconut oil
- 1 cup of nicely chopped unsweetened coconut (Optional ½ cup of unsweetened cocoa)

Directions

1. Diagonally slice the chocolate into little fragments. Combine in a bowl coconut oil and chocolate and put aside.
2. In a small saucepan, warm the coconut milk over medium heat and allow to simmer. After that, add the coconut milk on the coconut oil and chocolate and
2. Gently stir with a spatula to really blend well. It won't be okay to stir rigorously otherwise the chocolate can get grainy.
3. Bring in the vanilla concentrate and mix well.
4. Turn the chocolate mixture into a sealed bowl and keep for minimum 4 hours in the refrigerator to get strong.
5. Preheat oven to 300° F. Now, spread the chopped coconut onto a lined baking sheet and heat about for 4to 6 in the oven until it turns golden brown. Put the flakes on a shallow bowl once it's cooled. Assuming you're coating the truffles with cocoa powder, then pour some into a different bowl.
6. With a handy 1-inch disher or melon baller, scoop mixture to form balls of chocolate. Turn every one ball of chocolate with your palms to make an even ball
7. Cover each truffle ball with cocoa or toasted coconut and then shake off carefully excess.
8. Truffles could be stored in an airtight can for 7 days in a refrigerator or even up to three months in a freezer.
9. Never cover truffles with cocoa powder or chopped coconut if you want to store your truffles in the freezer until when you want to consume it. Preferably, leave under room temperature for about half an hour before coating. Then serve and enjoy!

Note: This recipe provides about 36 truffles

Bourbon Chocolate Truffles

Contents

- 2 tbsp of extreme whipping cream
- 2 freshly riped avocados, skinned and roughly cut
- ½ cup of diced pecans
- 1 cup of high quality cocoa powder
- 2 tbsp of coconut oil
- 1 tbsp of granulated sugar
- 2 tbsp of SF chocolate tasting syrup
- 2 tbsp of bourbon (recommended)

Directions

1. Add all the contents together in a food processor excluding the pecans until soft. Now, put in the freezer and chill for minimum 1 hour until sufficiently solid to work with.
2. Roll into one inch balls after which you fold in the pecans. Keep in the fridge to chill.

Coco-Cocoa Walnut Bark

Contents

- 2 tbsp of melted coconut oil
- 1 tbsp of powdered sugar
- 1 tbsp of unsweetened cocoa powder
- 1 tbsp cream, heavy whipping (homogenized)
- 1 tbsp of walnut halves, cut and toasted
- 1 dash salt

Instructions

1. Combine the cocoa powder with the melted coconut oil, cut walnuts, salt and sugar or its equivalent.
2. Stir in the cream until the entire mixture becomes fluffy smooth chocolaty sauce.
3. Spread onto 1/4-inch thick sheet of wax paper and then put in the fridge.
4. After it cools, serve and enjoy!

Coconut-Chocolate, Macadamia Nut Tart

Contents

For the Crust
- 1 ½ cups of almond flour
- ½ cup of unsweetened chopped coconut
- 2 tbsp of Maple Syrup
- 2 tbsp of coconut oil
- ¼ tsp of salt

For the Coconut Milk Ganache
- 1 cup of whole fat coconut milk
- 1 tsp of vanilla extract
- 280g bittersweet chocolate, thinly chopped

For the Topping
- 1 cup natural macadamia nuts, roughly cut
- 1/2 cup of unsweetened coconut flakes
- Dash of sea salt

Directions

Prepare Tart Coating
1. Preheat oven to 350o F. Combine together in a food processor the almond flour, chopped coconut and salt and blend into powder. Also mix together the coconut oil and maple syrup, then pour into the almond flour and add coconut mixture, blend until it becomes rough crumbs.
2. Move dough to an oiled 9inch tart pan that has detachable base. With a measuring cup or even your own fingers, uniformly press dough in the base and up edges of pan.
3. Put in the middle of oven and bake 16 to 22 minutes until golden brown. Put them on wire rack for 1 hour to completely cool.

Prepare The Topping
4. Uniformly scatter the chopped macadamia nuts as well as chopped coconut over a sheet Put in the oven and bake for about 4 to 6 minutes until slightly golden and keep aside.

To Prepare Ganache
5. Add the sliced chocolate into a big bowl. Also, boil the coconut milk in a small saucepan and pour this heated coconut milk on the chocolate, allow to sit for about a minute. Stir until glossy and creamy, add in vanilla concentrate.

Finally Piece Tart Together
6. Spread chocolate over the cooled tart layer. Gently spread the toasted macadamia nuts and also the toasted coconut on top. Splash some flaky sea salt if required.
7. Put in the fridge or freezer for the minimum, an hour to chill. Serve and enjoy!

2   Mexican Wedding Cookies

Contents
- 2 cups of almond flour
- 1 tbsp of maple syrup
- 1 cup of finely cut toasted pecans,
- Little sea salt
- 4 tbsp of extra virgin coconut oil
- 1/2 tsp of baking soda
- Seeds of one vanilla pod

Directions
1. Line your baking pan with parchment paper. Preheat oven to 175°C.
2. Combine all of the dry contents together in a sizable mixing container. After that, mix the wet ingredients and then consolidate the two mixtures and mix properly. Usually, if it's sticky enough then add more coconut oil.
3. With a tablespoon, scoop the dough and use your palms to press to make balls. You possibly can flatten them a bit on the base. Then set them on the baking sheet, bake up to 8 to 10 minutes.
4. Leave for 15 minutes to cool. Consume.

Vanilla Bean Truffles

Contents
- 1 cup of coconut butter (whole coconut cream extract)
- 1 vanilla bean
- 1/2 cup of coconut oil
- 1/2 cup of grade B maple syrup
- 2 teaspoons of natural vanilla extract
- 5 ounces of chocolate, for dipping

Directions
1. Dissolve the coconut oil together with coconut butter over low heat. Cut the vanilla bean lengthwise then take out all of the seeds and put in the seeds into the coconut butter fusion, add in the vanilla concentrate and also maple syrup. Mix to properly combine.
2. Put in the fridge and allow for about 20 minutes to solidify for molding.
3. Also you can mold the Truffles into hearts or even any form. Refrigerate until the molded truffles is cold.
4. Put chocolate in the microwave for 1 a minute or 2 minutes to dissolve. Bathe the truffle with dissolved chocolate and keep them on waxed paper for the chocolate solidifies on it. It yielded roughly 20 truffles and this is varying with the size.

Coconut Raspberry Fudge

Contents

- 1/2 Cup of dissolved Coconut oil
- 1/2 Cup of Raspberries
- 1/4 Cup of Honey
- 1/4 Cup of Unsweetened cocoa powder
- 1/4 Cup of Grass-fed Chocolate protein powder
- 1/4 tsp of Vanilla extract

Directions

1. Mix honey and coconut oil together in a microwave safe bowl and melt in a microwave oven.
2. Using fork, squash the raspberries in a pan
3. After the coconut oil dissolves, stir in the mashed raspberries, vanilla extract, Chocolate protein powder and unsweetened cocoa powder until properly mixed.
4. Line your baking sheet with parchment paper.
5. Fill pan with the mixture, then put in the freezer for about 40 minutes to 1 hour to solidify.
6. Cut and savor

Mango Banana Coconut Smoothie With Chia Seeds

Contents

- 1 cup of cubed iced mango
- 2 bananas
- 1 teaspoon of chia seeds
- 1 tablespoon of coconut oil
- 3/4 cup of coconut milk

Directions

1. Combine the bananas, coconut milk, coconut oil and mango into a blender and pulse until it's smooth.
2. You can increase the coconut milk till you get the expected texture. Finally, put in the chia seeds, beat for some time, then serve.

Paleo Carrot Cupcake

Contents
- 1.5 cups of white almond flour
- 1/2 teaspoon of nutmeg
- 1/2 teaspoon of baking soda
- 1 tsp of cinnamon
- 1 tsp of sea salt
- 2 tbsp of almond oil or alternatively grapeseed oil
- 1/4 teaspoon of cardamom
- 1/2 cup of pureed dates (If you opt for dried out dates they usually are extremely difficult to puree in the food processor, you can soften by heating with little water in the microwave, removed excess water after which puree)
- 1/4 cup of maple syrup
- 3 eggs
- 1 1/2 cups of thinly cut carrots (process with food processor)
- 1 cup of roughly cut pecans

Frosting Ingredients
- 1 cup of maple syrup
- 1 cup of coconut oil

Directions

1. Preheat oven to 325° F.
2. Now, mix together in a mixing bowl, the almond flour, baking soda, nutmeg, cardamom, cinnamon and salt.
3. Also combine in another bowl, the maple syrup, coconut oil and eggs and mix.
4. Now, stir in your dates and carrots into the moisten mixture.
5. Combine the wet mixture together with the dry mixtures
6. Tuck in the pecans.
7. Distribute equally into all 12 lined cupcake.
8. Put in the oven and bake for 23 minutes at 325o F until golden brown.

Frosting Instructions

1. Mix up the maple syrup and coconut oil together in a hand mixer until smooth.
2. Distribute frosting on all the cooled cupcakes.
3. Consume. Enjoy!

Strawberry Cupcakes with Strawberry Buttercream

Contents
- 1 cup of coconut flour
- 1/2 cup of coconut oil
- 1/4 teaspoon of sea salt
- 1/4 teaspoon of baking soda
- 4 eggs
- 2/3 cup of honey
- 3 tbsp fresh strawberry puree
- 1/4 cup of mashed fresh strawberries
- 2 tsp of vanilla
- Strawberry Buttercream Icing
- 1/2 tsp of vanilla
- 1/2 cup of unsalted butter
- 2 cups of icing sugar

Directions
1. Preheat oven to 350o.

For Strawberry Cupcakes:

2. Mix in a bowl the baking soda, coconut flour, add little salt.
3. Also, add together the coconut oil, vanilla, eggs and honey an a mixer until properly mixed.
4. Now, combine the flour mixture together with egg mixture and stir properly
5. Add in the strawberry puree.
6. Pour into cupcake about 3/4 full.
7. Bake in the preheated oven for 19 to 24 minutes, then remove and allow to totally cool before applying frosting.

For Strawberry Buttercream Icing

8. Pulse 4 strawberries and keep aside.
9. Sift the icing sugar.
10. Blend the butter with a mixer until smooth and creamy. Add in the sifted icing sugar, mix well to combine.
11. Incorporate strawberry puree and the vanilla.
12. After that, spread the frosting on top of cupcakes and then garnish with some slices of refreshing strawberry.

Peanut Butter Oatmeal Cookies With Cherries, Coconut and Dark Chocolate

Contents

- 4 tbsp of apple butter
- 1.1/2 cup of pure peanut butter
- 2 tbsp of dissolved coconut oil
- 1 cup of brown sugar
- 1/3 cup of sugar
- 2 tsp of vanilla extract
- ½ cup of unsweetened almond milk
- 1 1/2 tsp of baking soda
- 2 tbsp of cornstarch
- Dash of salt
- 1/3 cup of low fat unsweetened shredded coconut
- 6 oz of dark chocolate cut into chunks
- 3 cups of natural oats (gluten-free)
- 1 cup of roughly cut sweet cherries.

Instructions

1. Preheat your oven to 350°F. With silpat or parchment paper, line 2 baking sheets and set aside.

2. Whisk together in a big bowl the apple butter, peanut butter, sugars and coconut oil. Include baking soda, almond milk, cornstarch, vanilla, coconut and salt; whisk until properly mixed. Tuck in the oats along with cherries, coconut and chocolate.

3. Scoop the mixture with a small cookie scooper onto the lined baking sheet and give them separate from each other about 2 inches. .

4. Put in the oven and bake for about 10 to 15 minutes until the sides turn golden brown.

Remarks: Such cookies can be very gooey and it's not recommended to seal them.

Coconut-Macadamia Nut Waffles

Contents

- 2 cups of high quality General Flour
- 2 cup of coconut milk
- 1 tsp of baking powder
- 1 cup of club soda
- 1/2 tsp of salt
- 2 eggs
- 1/3 cup of roasted macadamia nuts, diced
- 1 tsp of vanilla extract
- 1/4 cup of vegetable oil (alternatively coconut oil)
- 1/3 cup of shredded coconut
- You can top with Beaten Cream, Macadamia Nuts, Coconut and Maple Syrup.

Instructions

1. Stir together in a bowl the flour, salt and baking powder, add in the vanilla, club soda, coconut milk, coconut oil and eggs together with the nuts and shredded coconut.
2. Preheat your waffle container in the oven.
3. Grease the sides of the waffle plates with non-stick baking oil. Now scoop the waffle mixture into the waffle plates, close the lids.
4. Bake for about 5 minutes.
5. Top with additional coconut and macadamia nuts, then the beaten cream and syrup.
6. Server.

Handmade Granola Bars

Contents
- 5 cups whole oats
- 1 cup of fresh cashews, chopped
- 1 cup of natural almonds, chopped
- 2/3 cup of unsweetened shredded coconut
- 1/2 cup of natural pepitas
- 1/3 cup of sesame seeds
- 1/2 cup of dried cranberries
- 1/2 cup of raisins
- 1/2 cup of honey
- 1/2 cup of brown sugar (alternatively use palm sugar)
- 2 tbsp of vanilla concentrate
- 1/2 cup of brown rice syrup
- 1/2 cup of coconut oil
- 1/2 tsp of sea salt

Instructions
1. Put about 2cups of oats in a mixer and beat until nicely ground.
2. Now, mix together in a big bowl the leftover whole oats, the grounded oat, coconut, nuts, dried fruits and seeds.
3. Line a big 13 by 18" rimmed baking pan with wax paper.
4. Combine together in a saucepan the brown rice syrup, coconut oil, brown sugar and honey, then place on high heat let it heat up and stir very well. Remove from heat and add salt and vanilla. Pour this mixture on the dry ingredients.
5. Stir properly to ensure that the dry ingredients are properly coated, after that, pour batter onto baking pan and spread uniformly. Put in the fridge for about 1 to 2 hours for it to set.
6. Once it's set, cut into squares. Enclose well in a wrapper then keep in the fridge until when you want to serve.

German Chocolate Cheesecake

Contents

For the crust
- 3 tbsp of melted coconut oil
- 10 ozs of chocolate sandwich cookies

For the cheesecake
- 9 ozs of low fat cream cheese
- 9 ozs of no fat cream cheese
- 3 tbsp of unsweetened cocoa powder
- 7 ozs of dark chocolate (or Baker's German chocolate)
- 1/2 cup of brown sugar
- 1 tsp of almond concetrate
- 6 eggs kept at room temperature.
- 1 tsp of vanilla extract

For the coconut topping
- 1 cup of shredded coconut
- 1 tsp of vanilla extract
- 6 tbsp of coconut oil
- 1/3 cup of brown sugar
- 1 cup of whole fat canned coconut milk
- 1/2 tsp of almond extract
- ½ tsp of bourbon (optional)

Directions

1. Grease with nonstick oil a 10" springform baking pan and wrap tightly the outer side of the baking pan with tinfoil. And preheat oven to 350o F.
2. Blend in a food processor the chocolate sandwich cookies until they turn into fine small crumbs. Gently add in coconut oil and then press down the crust into the base of the baking pan. Put in the oven and bake for 8 minutes, remove and allow to cool.
3. In a large bowl, whisk together the cream cheese, brown sugar and the melted chocolate until properly mixed. Add in the eggs, almond extracts and vanilla, continue whisking until fully incorporated.
4. Combine the cheesecake mixture and the crust. Let it sit in a big pan filled with water about 1/3 full. Put in the oven and bake for about 45 minutes. Remove and allow for 40 minutes to cool before frosting.
5. Now prepare coconut topping by mixing together in a saucepan the brown sugar, coconut oil, coconut milk and shredded coconut. Let it boil, lower the heat and continue to stir for 4 minutes until it coagulates. Spread it over the cooled cheesecake. You can spread more liquid chocolate and if required top with toasted coconut. Cover and refrigerate for 3hours. Serve and Enjoy.

Coconut Whole Wheat Tortillas

Contents
- 3 cups of whole wheat flour, (split in two)
- 1/3 cup of coconut oil
- 1 tsp of sea salt
- 1 cup of hot water

Directions
1. Add 2.1/2 cups of flour, coconut oil and salt into a mixing bowl, mix to combine the oil very well and until dough seems crisp.
2. Carefully stream in hot water while mixer is running at low speed, keep mixing for about 4 minutes until the batter is wet and properly combined.
3. Move dough onto a floured sheet and then knead even as you add the leftover flour until dough is smooth and soft.
4. Cut dough into twelve or more pieces depending on size, then roll to form balls. After that keep somewhere and cover for about 1 hour or two.
5. Place non-stick pan or cast iron on medium to high heat, fill pan with oil for frying tortilla. As the pan is heating, roll dough balls on a lightly floured sheet and then press to flatten until very lean.
6. Put tortillas into the hot pan to fry for 3 minutes. Turn the other side and cook for another 2 minutes. Remove from heat and repeat with the remaining ones until you finish them. Note: Preserve in a closed zip top bag. Serve when ready.

Paleo Sweet Potato for Breakfast Hash

Contents
- 1 sizable sweet potato cut into pieces
- 2 tbsp of coconut oil
- ½ lb medium cut bacon
- 1 tbsp of olive oil
- 1 small cut onion
- 1/2 tsp of salt and pepper
- 4 eggs (Eggland's Best)

Directions
1. On medium heat, place your large pan and add coconut oil. Add in sweet potatoes, pepper, salt and olive oil; stir frequently and fry until slightly brown, add onions and stir for few minutes.
2. Lower the heat, loosely cover with aluminum foil and allow to simmer for 14 minutes until sweet potatoes is soft.
3. Move sweet potatoes to one corner of the pan, raise the heat and add bacon to the cleared out space, frequently stirring it, fry for 8 minutes until crunchy. Ensure you also stir the sweet potatoes to avoid burning. After the bacon is cooked, then lower heat to low, add in all the other ingredients.
4. Remove from heat and fry your eggs any how you want it. Serve hash and top with fried eggs. The remaining if any might be put in an airtight bowl and refrigerate though without egg.

Coconut Oil Mango Banana Peach Bread

Contents

- 2 sizable eggs
- 1 of coconut oil (canola or vegetable is okay)
- 1/3 cup of sour cream (or Greek yogurt)
- 1 cup of light brown sugar, packed
- 1 tbsp of vanilla extract
- 4 big ripped bananas, mashed
- 2 cups of general flour
- 1 tsp of baking powder
- 1 teaspoon of baking soda
- little salt to taste
- 2 cups of chopped mangoes-peach mixture. ratio depends as you like (alternatively use strawberries, nectarines or blueberries)
- 3 tbsp of general purpose flour, for coating peach-mangoes

Instructions

1. Oil 2 or more loaf pans and sprinkle with flour, keep aside. Preheat the oven to 350o F.
2. Combine all these together in a big bowl, the brown sugar, coconut oil, eggs, vanilla and sour cream, beat to mix very well.
3. Put in the bananas and continue to stir to mix properly.
4. Bring in the 2 cups of flour, baking soda, salt, baking powder and then mix properly but never overmix.
5. Mix together in another small bowl, the mangoes and peaches with 3 tbsp of flour and stir to coat in order to avoid the fruits depressing.
6. Now tuck the mangos-peaches into the mixture.
7. Fill the prepared pans with the mixture and carefully smoothing the tops with a spoon as well as pressing it into corners if required.
8. Put in the oven and bake for 43 minutes or until the top is golden and vaulted. Test the middle with a toothpick and if it comes out clean, then remove from heat. Note baking time may vary depending on the mangoes, peaches and bananas moisture contents as well the type of oven.
9. Remove from oven and allow for about 10 to 17 minutes to cool before you bring bread out from pan, leave on the wire rack to completely cool. Then slice and enjoy!
10. Optional, you can serve bread Cinnamon-Sugar Butter, Strawberry Butter, Blueberry Butter or Honey Butter.

Drunken Noodles

Contents

For the Sauce
- 1/2 cup of oyster sauce
- 2 tbsp of brown sugar
- 2 tbsp of fresh lime juice
- 1/2 cup of fish sauce
- 2 tbsp Maggi Sauce (or Golden Mountain)

For the Drunken Noodles:
- 1 lb of chicken breast, cut to bits
- 1 lb of DeLallo Egg Noodles (or rice noodles)
- 3 eggs, beaten
- 4 cloves garlic, minced
- 2 thai chiles (or 2 jalapeños)
- 1 small onion, cut
- 1 cup of shredded carrots
- 1 cup of red bell pepper, remove seed and diced
- 1 cup of green onion tops, cut to pieces
- 1 cup of loose thai basil leaves
- 1 cup of grape tomatoes cut into half
- Coconut oil for cooking
- Lime wedges for garnish

Instructions

1. In a small dish, mix the sauce together. Put the cut chicken breast into a different container, add 3 tbsp of sauce and mix to marinade.

2. Cut the remaining ingredients and keep aside. Cook noodles following the package instructions.

3. Now place your pot on a high heat, add about one tbsp of oil into the pot and scramble the eggs. Shove the eggs to one side; add garlic, onions and thai chiles and stir for few minutes. Bring in the chicken, add one tbsp of oil if necessary and continue to stir while it's frying for about 5 minutes until just nearly cooked. Move the cooked chicken mixture into a different pan and leave pan on heat.

4. At this point add the carrots and bell peppers and stir for few minutes, combine all the ingredients together and then pour in the noodles mix in the leftover sauce, green onions, tomatoes and thai basil. Stir for few minutes and remove from heat.

5. Serve warm and top with lime wedges

Homemade Kettle Corn Snack

Contents
- 1 cup of popcorn kernels
- 1/4 cup of sugar
- 1/2 cup of (Any good quality oil will do)
- 1/4 tsp of salt
- 1/2 tsp of cayenne pepper (optional)

Instructions
1. Into a large heavy-base pot that has lid, pour the oil and popcorn kernels, shake to mix the oil and the popcorn kernel very well. Cover pot with lid, open the vent but In case the lid does not have a vent, then misalign the lid slightly to give small opening.
2. Set the pot on medium heat; allow the kernels to begin to pop. Now, measure out the salt and sugar and keep aside.
3. When kernels popping starts reducing, open pot and then add salt, sugar and cayenne and switch off heat, while the popcorn is still hot, shake the pot in a circular motion to mix up the ingredients together and coat the popcorn. Serve or keep popcorn in an air-tight can for as long as you want.

Rich Feta & Leek Piled Crepes with Roasted Red Pepper Sauce

Contents

Filling Ingredients
- 3 tbsp of butter
- 3 cups of leeks (rinse & cut)
- 2 .1/2 tbsp of sherry
- ¼ tsp of salt
- 4 tbsp of mascarpone
- 1 ounce of goat cheese
- 7 ounces of feta cheese, crumbled
- 1/3 teaspoon of dry basil leaves
- 2 cups of cherry tomatoes (split into 2)

Crepes Ingredients
- 1 cup of flour
- 1 cup of water
- 2 eggs
- ¼ tsp of salt
- 1 cup of milk
- 3 tbsp of melted coconut oil

For the sauce
- 1 small onion, thinly chopped
- 1 cup of roasted red pepper
- 1 tbsp of olive oil
- 1/2 cup of water
- 1 garlic clove, minced
- 1 tsp of apple cider vinegar
- ¼ tsp of salt
- 1 tsp of sugar
- Red pepper flakes (optional)

Directions

Preheat the oven to 350 o.

For the crepes:
1. Mix together in a bowl, the salt and flour, use a different bowl to combine together the coconut oil, eggs, milk and water, now mix the two together and thoroughly blend until properly mixed. Keep aside.
2. Add 1 tablespoon of coconut oil into the non-stick pan, spin and place on heat.
3. Scoop mixture out with a cup, lift the pan off heat with your left hand and use the other hand to immediately pour the scooped mixture into skillet then slant skillet and rotate in a circular form, to let the mixture fill the base of the skillet.
4. When the sides get somewhat crispy or golden brown, turn the other side and allow cooking for extra 25 seconds.
5. Prepare all the leftover crepes.

For the filling:

1. Over medium heat, dissolve butter in a non-stick pan. Put in the leeks, salt and allow cooking for 5 minutes to become light and soft. Add basil and sherry and let it simmer a little, then add cheeses. Mix until goat cheese and mascarpone dissolves and feta roughly melts. Remove from heat and keep.

2. Now set one crepe over the other and distribute the leek and feta filling on top crepes Put half of the cherry tomatoes randomly on the filling. Place another two more crepes on top, and then the sherry tomatoes. Do this again, however on the final layer place with a single crepe.

3. Move them to a lined baking tray and bake until filling is really hot and the tomato is soft.

4. Now, prepare the sauce. Put the roasted red peppers into a food processor and blend.

5. Heat oil in a small saucepan on a medium heat, add in onion and garlic and stir until soft. Pour in the pureed red peppers, vinegar, salt, red pepper flakes, sugar and water. Then allow cooking for about 9 minutes. Remove from heat.

6. You can cut crepes into any pieces you want and serve with roasted red pepper sauce topping.

Vietnamese Banh Mi Street Tacos

Contents

For the Vietnamese Banh Mi Chicken
- 4 garlic cloves, minced
- 2 tbsp of coconut oil
- 1 jalapeno
- 1 cup of fresh lime juice
- 1/2 cup of fish sauce
- 2 lbs of skinned boneless chicken laps
- 1/4 cup of granulated sugar

For the Spicy Mayo
- 3/4 cup of mayonnaise
- 1 tbsp of granulated sugar
- 3 tbsp of sriracha
- 1 tbsp of rice vinegar

For the Street Tacos
- 2 packs of Old El Paso Flour Tortillas (taco size)
- 4 jalapenos, cut
- 1 chopped English cucumber
- 3 cut carrots
- 2 bunches of chopped radishes
- A handful of cilantro or fresh mint
- 2 limes, cut into wedges

Instructions

1. Combine the lime juice, fish sauce and sugar together in an oven safe dish and put in the heated microwave for just few minutes for the sugar to melt. Cut into small bits the chicken thighs and put in a bowl, add in garlic and the cut jalapeno. Mix properly and keep in the fridge and about an hour or more.

2. To Prepare Spicy Mayo: Mix sugar and rice vinegar together in an oven safe dish and then microwave for few minutes to let sugar melt, add in sriracha and mayonnaise, then refrigerate.

3. To make the veggies. Heat a sizable pan on medium to high heat, put 2 tablespoon coconut oil, once it hot, add the marinated chicken and toast for about 6 minutes even as you keep mixing it to caramelize the chicken.

4. Scoop chicken into an Old El Paso flour tortillas and serve with sliced jalapeno, radishes, slices of cucumber, fresh mint leaves and the chopped carrots, apply fresh lime wedges and some spicy mayo on top.

Curried Carrot and Coconut Soup

Contents
- 2 tbsp of coconut oil
- 4 tsp of red curry paste
- 2 lbs of carrots, peeled and cut into big chunks
- 4 cups low-sodium chicken stock
- 1 mid size onions, chopped
- 2 tsp of salt, split
- 1 13-ounce light coconut milk

Directions
1. Add the coconut oil a large skillet and place over a medium heat, once it dissolves and hot, the add onions, carrot and a dash of salt, stir until a bit soft, then add curry paste and allow to simmer for a minute. Bring in the chicken stock and season to taste. Let it boil, then lower the heat, cover and allow for 13 minutes to cook.
2. Pour mixture into a mixer and pulse, then put back in the pot and then put in the leftover salt together with coconut milk and allow cooking for about 3 minutes and removing from heat.
3. Serve.

Printed in Great Britain
by Amazon